Introduction

The goal of this book is to increase the Hindi vocabulary of a child who is familiar with the English language and understands the basics of Hindi alphabet.

In the process of learning Hindi, this activity book would be the second in the *Learn Hindi series* of activity books. The first activity book introduced the basics of Hindi alphabet through a set of games and activities. This activity book builds the vocabulary by another set of puzzles and activities.

The vocabulary is introduced in many different groups. For each group, a set of related words are provided. The child performs matching games, finds the words in a maze, or matches pictures against words to learn the words and their meaning.

And since Hindi is phonetic, you can take any word in English and write it down in Hindi according to its sounds. Many items that were first discovered in Europe or the United States are used in Hindi that way, examples being computer, rail, train, and engine.

In this book, we have provided English transliteration of all Hindi words to help the child learn the pronunciation. To keep things easy and fun, we have tried to transliterate it to approximate the sounds which a casual reader will follow, instead of using a strict pedantic transliteration style. Since transliterating the exact sound of Hindi words in English is difficult, it is one area that talking to a Hindi speaker would be a good complement to the material in this book.

Apart from the pronunciation part, all you need to do is to hand over a set of crayons to your child with this book and see how it turns learning Hindi into an enjoyable affair.

Chanda Books
Email: chandabooks@optonline.net
Web: http://www.chandabooks.com

Published by arrangement with Create Space Publishing

Table of Contents

Hindi Alphabet/वर्णमाला

The Hindi Alphabet consists of 13 vowels and 33 consonants. The sounds of Hindi are made by combining the consonants with the vowels. The base vowel अ is implicit in each sound made by a consonant.

Vowels (स्वर)

अ आ इ ई उ ऊ ऋ ए ऐ ओ औ अं अः

Consonants (व्यंजन)

क ख ग घ ङ
च छ ज झ ञ
ट ठ ड ढ ण
त थ द ध न
प फ ब भ म
य र ल व
श ष स ह

When a consonant is combined with a vowel other than अ, a new sound is produced which is a modified version of the base sound of the consonant. The modified sound is shown by a mark called a matra (मात्रा). The matras for क combined with all of the vowels in sequence are:

क का कि की कु कू कृ के कै को कौ कं कः

There are special symbols for combinations of consonants to make new sounds. Some commonly used combinations are क्ष (क्+ष), त्र(त्+र), ज्ञ(ज्+ञ) and श्र (श्+र).

The tables for matras and consonant combinations are provided at the end of this book.

Greetings/सम्बोधन

Match these greetings in Hindi with their English equivalent by drawing a line from the greeting to the English phrase.

Hindi	English
1. नमस्ते (*namaste*)	A. I take your leave now
2. माफ कीजिये (*maaf keejiye*)	B. See you later
3. आप कैसे हैं? (*aap kaise hain*)	C. How are you?
4. मैं अच्छा हूँ (*main acchaa hoon*)	D. Hello/Goodbye
5. फिर मिलेंगे (*phir milenge*)	E. Excuse me
6. अब हम चलते हैं (*ab hum chalate hain*)	F. I am fine
7. धन्यवाद (*dhanyavaad*)	G. Thank you

Answers:
1. D
2. E
3. C
4. F
5. B
6. A
7. G

Reading & Writing/पढ़ना-लिखना

Match these items used in reading and writing with their pictures by drawing a line between the two.

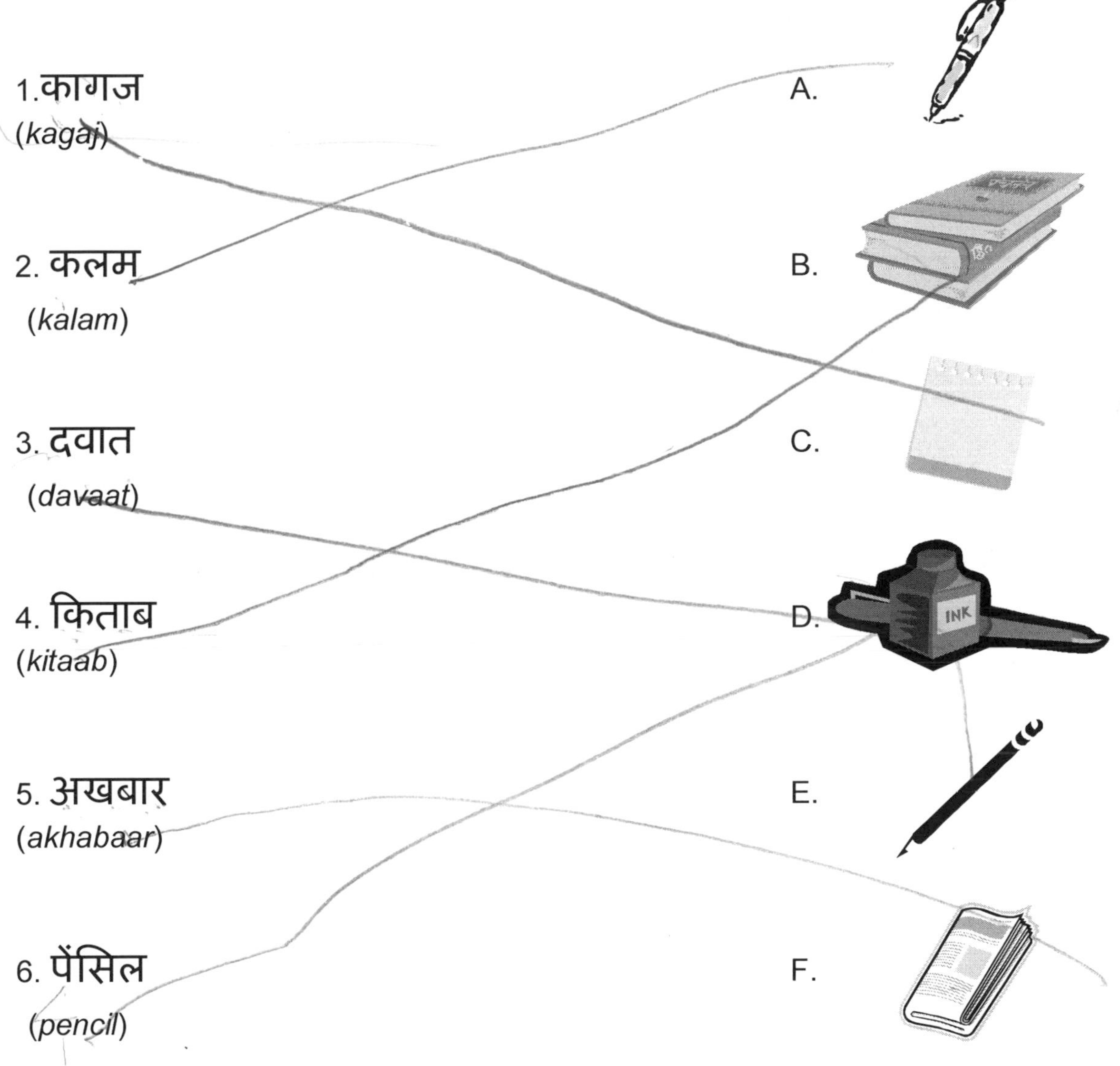

Answers:
1. C
2. A
3. D
4. B
5. F
6. E

Reading & Writing/पढ़ना-लिखना

Match these words in Hindi with their English equivalent by drawing a line between the Hindi word and its corresponding English word.

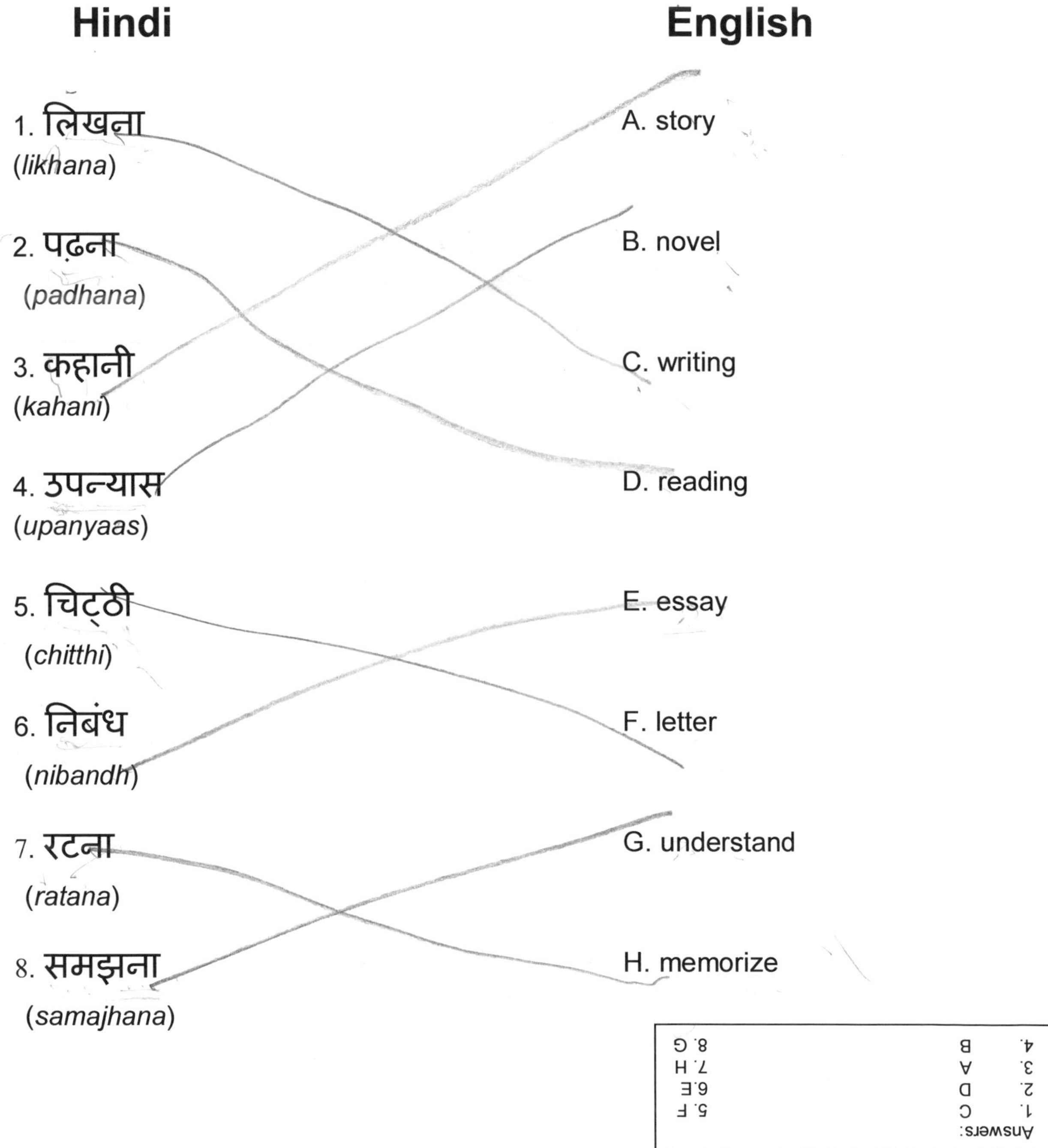

Hindi	English
1. लिखना (*likhana*)	A. story
2. पढ़ना (*padhana*)	B. novel
3. कहानी (*kahani*)	C. writing
4. उपन्यास (*upanyaas*)	D. reading
5. चिट्ठी (*chitthi*)	E. essay
6. निबंध (*nibandh*)	F. letter
7. रटना (*ratana*)	G. understand
8. समझना (*samajhana*)	H. memorize

Answers:
1. C
2. D
3. A
4. B
5. F
6.E
7. H
8. G

Pronoun/सर्वनाम

On the lines in the inner wheel, write the numbers from the list below that gives the name of the pronoun written on the corresponding outer wheel.

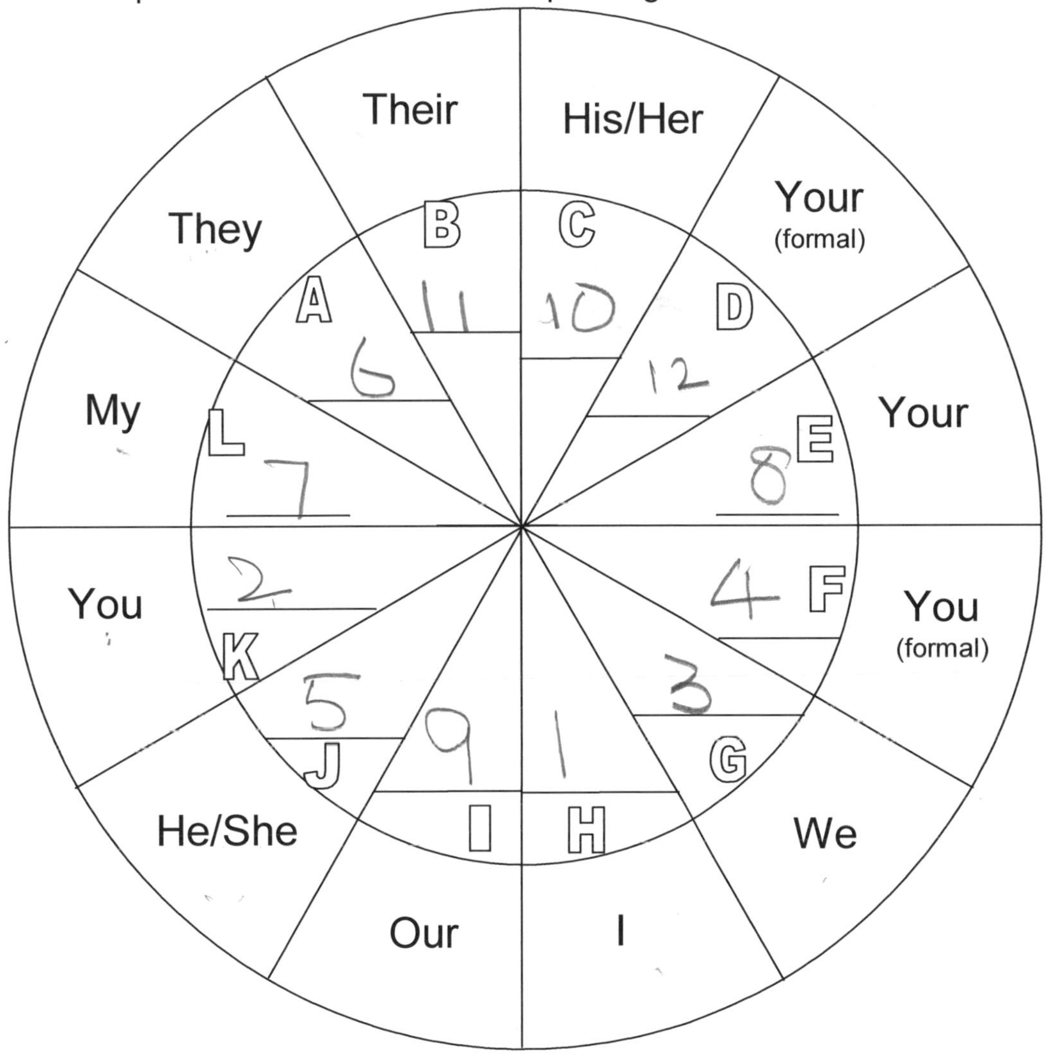

सूची (List)		
1. मैं (main)	5. वह (vah)	9. हमारा (hamaaraa)
2. तुम (tum)	6. वो (vo)	10. उसका (usakaa)
3. हम (hum)	7. मेरा (mera)	11.उनका (unakaa)
4. आप (aap)	8. तेरा (tera)	12. आपका (aapkaa)

Answer: 1. H 2. K 3. G 4. F 5. J 6. A 7. L 8. E 9. I 10. C 11. B 12. D

Pronoun/सर्वनाम

Match these words in Hindi with their English equivalent by drawing a line from the Hindi word to its corresponding English word.

Hindi	English
1. कौन (*kaun*)	A. What
2. क्यों (*kyon*)	B. Where
3. कहाँ (*kahaan*)	C. Who
4. क्या (*kya*)	D. Why
5. कोई (*koi*)	E. Everyone
6. सब (*sab*)	F. Someone
7. यहाँ (*yahaan*)	G. This
8. वहाँ (*vahaan*)	H. That
9. जहाँ (*jahaan*)	I. Here
10. यह (*yah*)	J. There
11. वह (*vah*)	K. Wherever

Answers:
1. C
2. D
3.B
4.A
5.F
6.E
7.I
8.J
9.K
10.G
11.H

Numbers/संख्या

Match the Hindi words in the middle columns below to the corresponding numbers in outer columns by drawing a line between them.

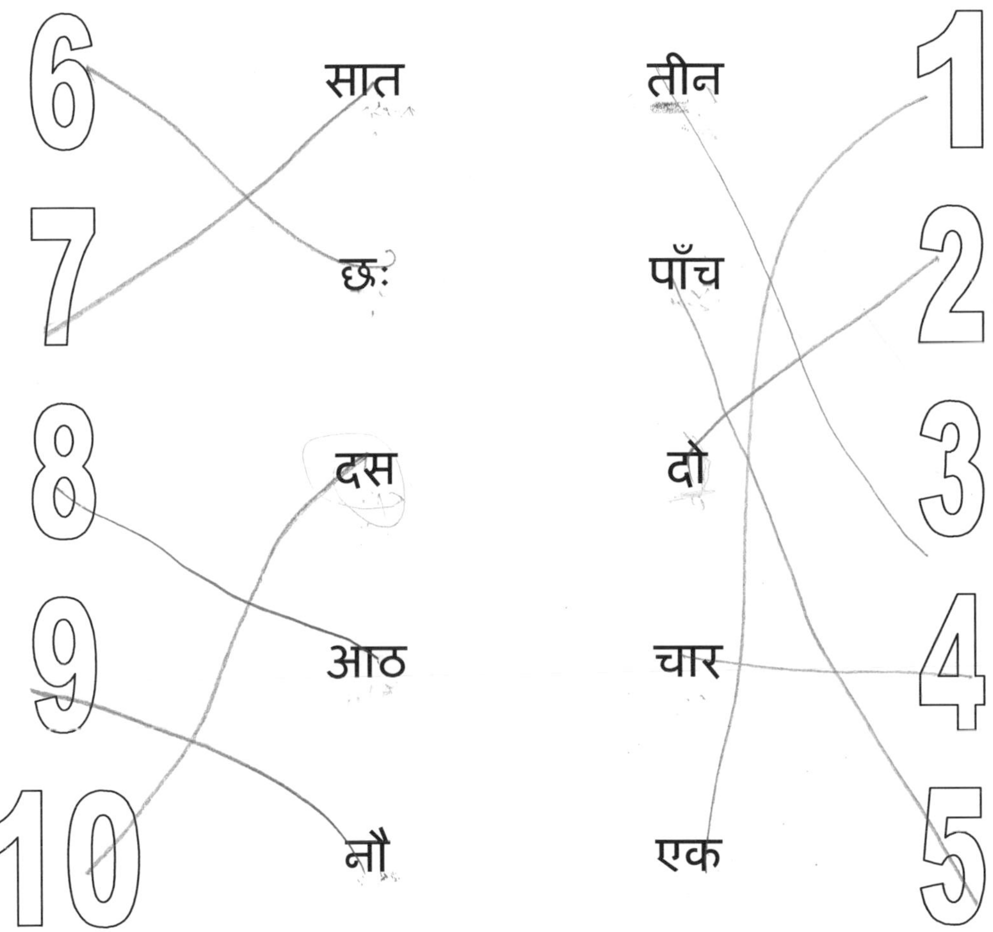

Table						
Hindi	Transliteration	English		Hindi	Transliteration	English
एक	eyk	one		छः	chhah	six
दो	do	two		सात	saat	seven
तीन	teen	three		आठ	aath	eight
चार	chaar	four		नौ	nau	nine
पाँच	paanch	five		दस	das	ten

Numbers/संख्या

Match the Hindi words in the middle columns below to the corresponding numbers in outer columns by drawing a line between them.

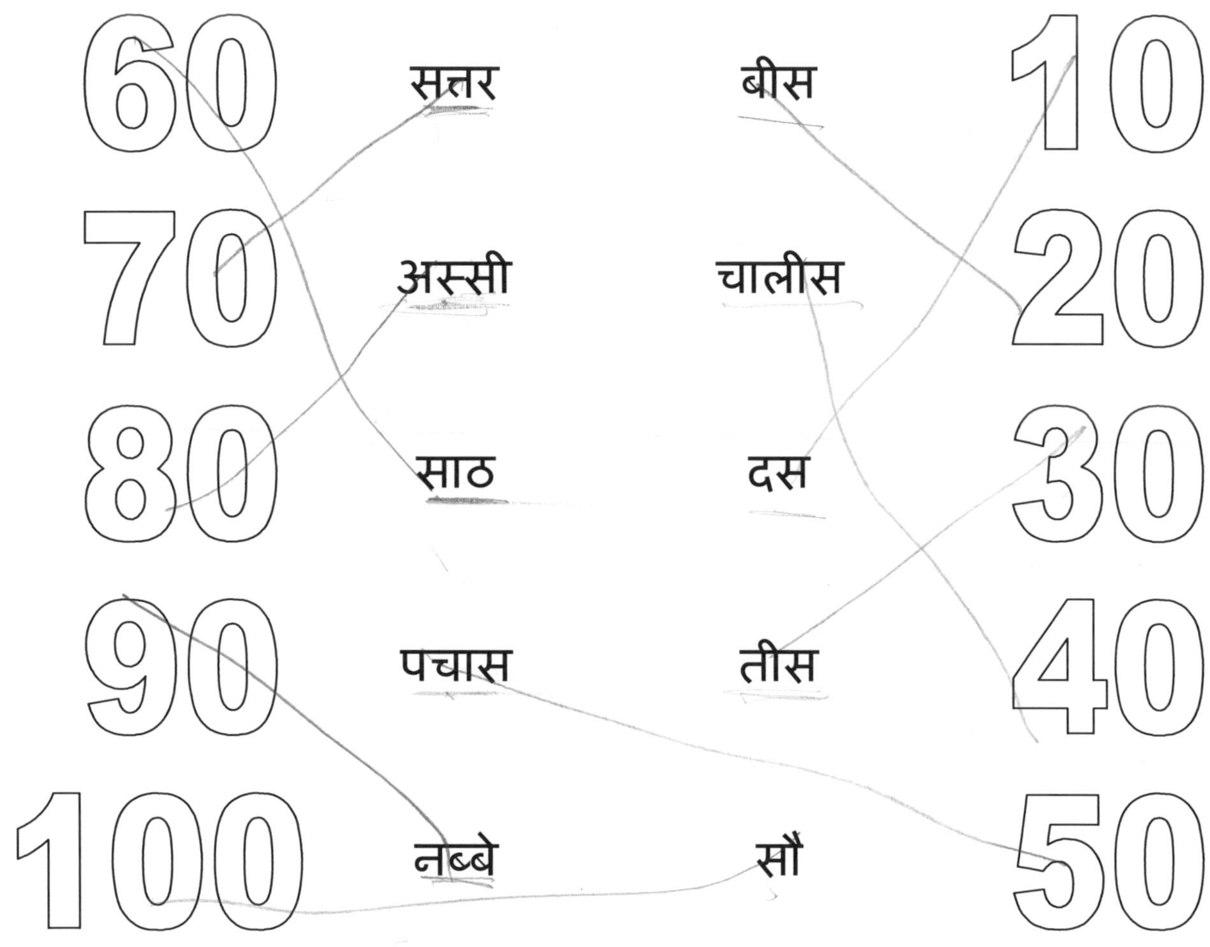

Table						
Hindi	Transliteration	English		Hindi	Transliteration	English
दस	das	ten		साठ	saath	sixty
बीस	bees	twenty		सत्तर	sattar	seventy
तीस	tees	thirty		अस्सी	assi	eighty
चालीस	chaarlees	forty		नब्बे	nabbe	ninety
पचास	pachaas	fifty		सौ	sau	hunder

Numbers/संख्या

Write the numbers on the lines in the inner wheel corresponding to Hindi words on the rim of this wheel, like the two examples shown.

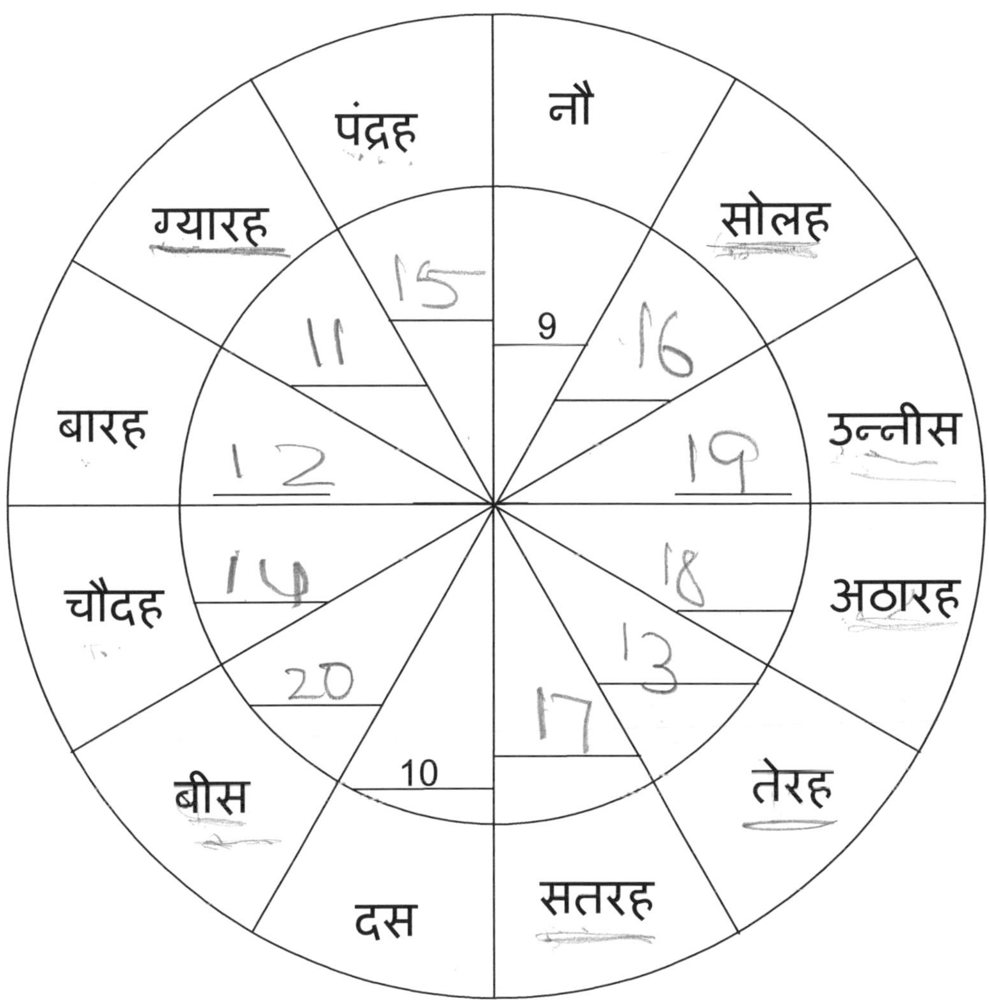

Table					
Hindi	Transliteration	English	Hindi	Transliteration	English
ग्यारह	gyaarah	11	सोलह	solah	16
बारह	baarah	12	सतरह	satarah	17
तेरह	terah	13	अठारह	athaarah	18
चौदह	chaudah	14	उन्नीस	unnees	19
पंद्रह	pandrah	15	बीस	bees	20

Numbers/संख्या

Match the Hindi words in the middle columns below to the corresponding numbers in outer columns by drawing a line between them.

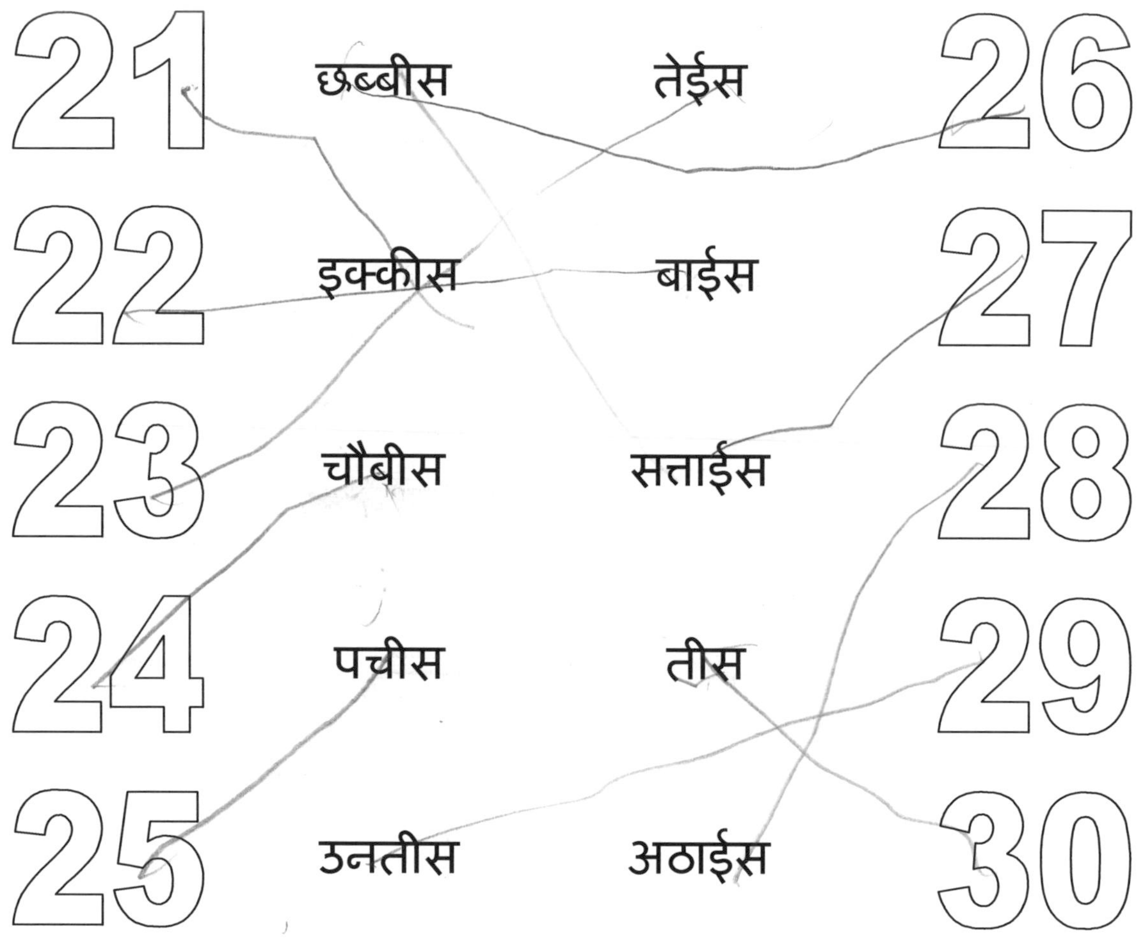

Table

Hindi	Transliteration	English		Hindi	Transliteration	English
इक्कीस	ekkis	21		छब्बीस	chabbees	26
बाईस	baaees	22		सत्ताईस	sattaees	27
तेईस	teyees	23		अठाईस	athhayees	28
चौबीस	chaubees	24		उनतीस	untees	29
पचीस	pachees	25		तीस	tees	30

Numbers/संख्या

Write the numbers on the lines in the inner wheel corresponding to Hindi words on the rim of this wheel, like the two examples shown.

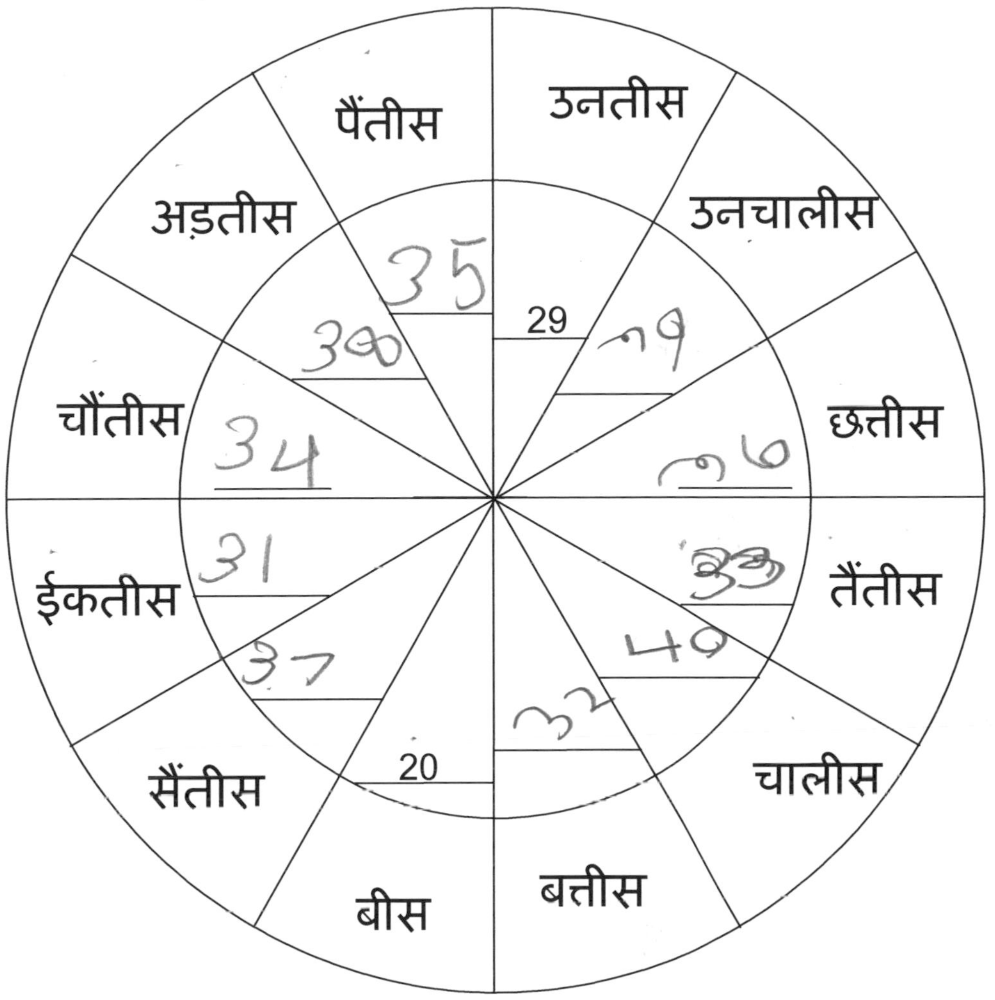

Table

Hindi	Transliteration	English		Hindi	Transliteration	English
ईकतीस	eyktees	31		छत्तीस	chattees	36
बत्तीस	battees	32		सैंतीस	saintees	37
तैंतीस	tyentees	33		अड़तीस	adatees	38
चौंतीस	chauntees	34		उनचालीस	unchaalees	39
पैंतीस	pantees	35		चालीस	chaalees	40

Numbers/संख्या

Match the Hindi words in the middle columns below to the corresponding numbers in outer columns by drawing a line between them.

Table						
Hindi	Transliteration	English		Hindi	Transliteration	English
एकतालिस	eyktaalis	41		छियालिस	chiyaalis	46
बयालिस	bayaalis	42		सैंतालिस	santaalis	47
तैंतालिस	tyentalis	43		अड़तालिस	adtaalis	48
चौवालिस	chauvalis	44		उनचास	unchaas	49
पैंतालिस	pantalis	45		पचास	pachaas	50

Numbers/संख्या

Write the numbers on the lines in the inner wheel corresponding to Hindi words on the rim of this wheel, like the two examples shown.

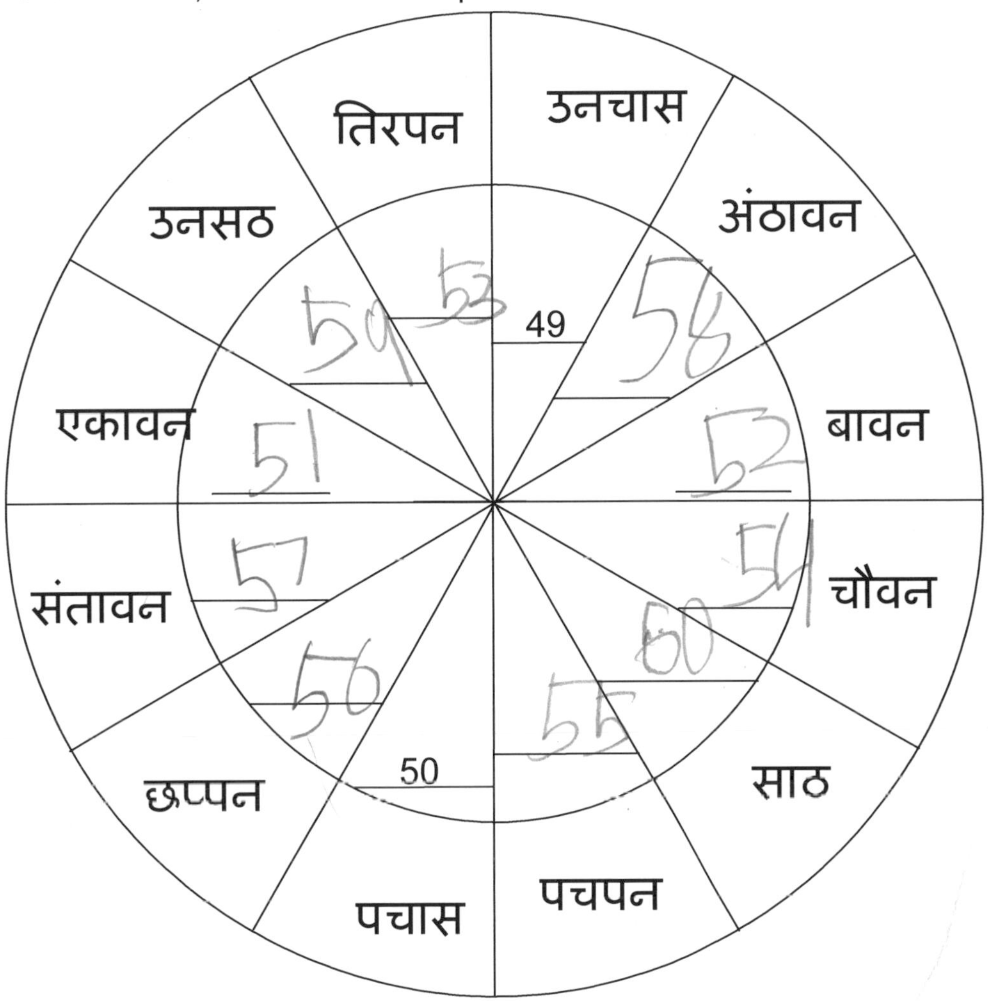

Table						
Hindi	Transliteration	English		Hindi	Transliteration	English
एकावन	eykavan	51		छप्पन	chappan	56
बावन	bavan	52		संतावन	santaavan	57
तिरपन	tirpan	53		अंठावन	anthaavan	58
चौवन	chauvan	54		उनसठ	unsath	59
पचपन	pachpan	55		साठ	saath	60

Numbers/संख्या

Write the numbers on the lines in the inner wheel corresponding to Hindi words on the rim of this wheel, like the two examples shown.

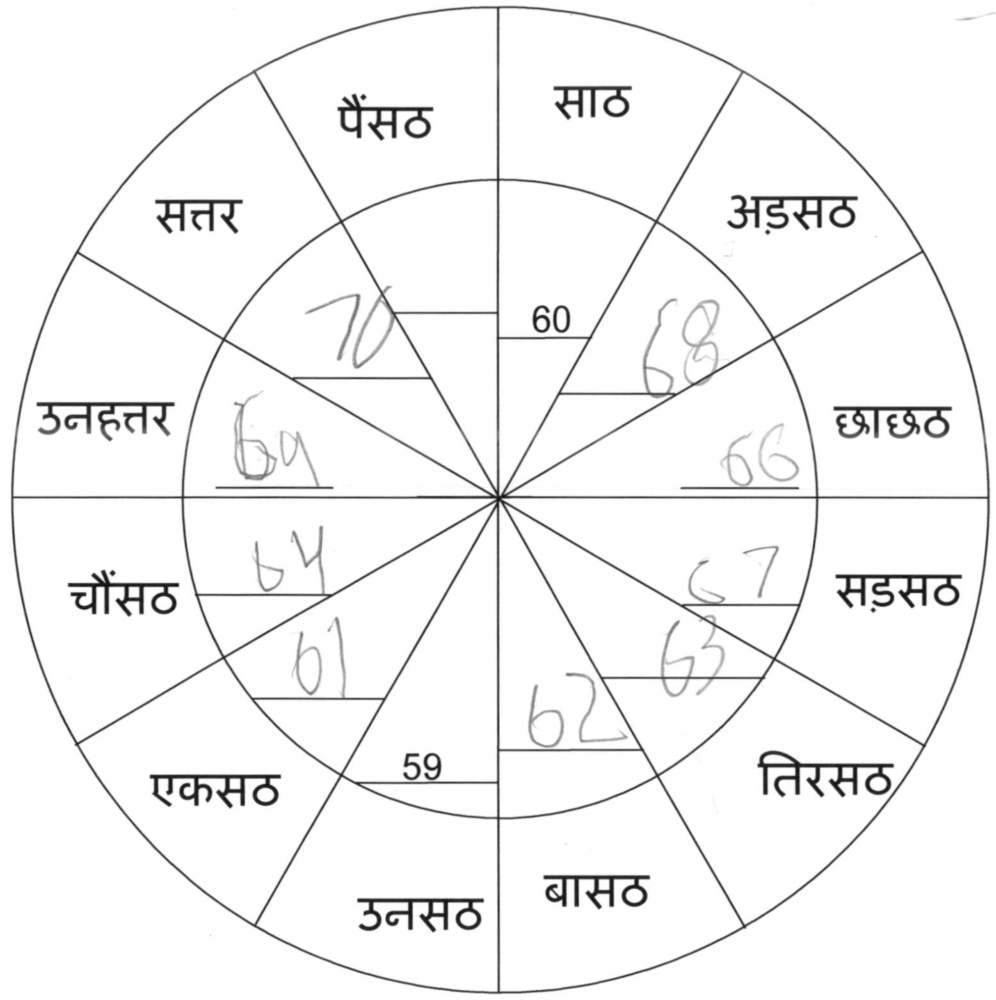

Table						
Hindi	Transliteration	English		Hindi	Transliteration	English
एकसठ	eyksath	61		छाछठ	chaachath	66
बासठ	baasath	62		सड़सठ	sadhasath	67
तिरसठ	tirsath	63		अड़सठ	adhasath	68
चौंसठ	chaunsath	64		उनहत्तर	unhattar	69
पैंसठ	painsath	65		सत्तर	sattar	70

Numbers/संख्या

Match the Hindi words in the middle columns below to the corresponding numbers in outer columns by drawing a line between the two.

Table						
Hindi	Transliteration	English		Hindi	Transliteration	English
एकहत्तर	eykhattar	71		छिहत्तर	chhihattar	76
बहत्तर	bahattar	72		सतहत्तर	satahattar	77
तिहत्तर	tihattar	73		अठहत्तर	adahattar	78
चौहत्तर	chauhattar	74		उनासी	unaasee	79
पचहत्तर	pachahattar	75		अस्सी	assee	80

Numbers/संख्या

Write the numbers on the lines in the inner wheel corresponding to Hindi words on the rim of this wheel, like the two examples shown.

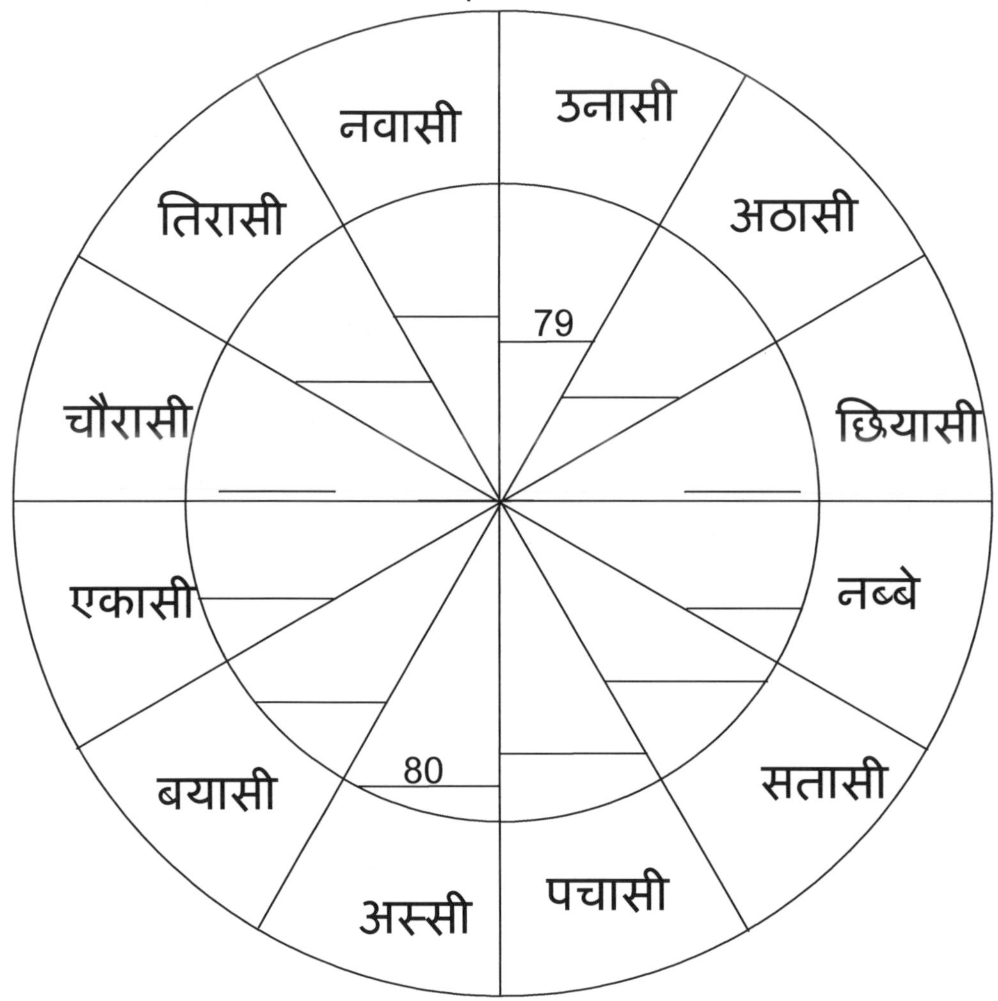

Table						
Hindi	Transliteration	English		Hindi	Transliteration	English
एकासी	eykaasee	81		छियासी	chhiyaasee	86
बयासी	bayaasee	82		सतासी	sataasee	87
तिरासी	tiraasee	83		अठासी	athasee	88
चौरासी	chauraasee	84		नवासी	navaasee	89
पचासी	pachaasee	85		नब्बे	nabbe	90

Numbers/संख्या

Match the Hindi words in the middle columns below to the corresponding numbers in outer columns by drawing a line between them.

91	छियानबे	तिरानबे	96
92	एकानबे	बानबे	97
93	चौरानबे	संतानबे	98
94	पंचानबे	सौ	99
95	निनांबे	अंठानबे	100

Table

Hindi	Transliteration	English		Hindi	Transliteration	English
एकानबे	eykaanabey	91		छियानबे	chhiyaanabey	96
बानबे	baanabey	92		संतानबे	santaanabey	97
तिरानबे	tiraanabey	93		अंठानबे	anthaanabey	98
चौरानबे	chauraanabey	94		निनांबे	ninaanabey	99
पंचानबे	panchaanabey	95		सौ	sau	100

Numbers/संख्या

Match the Hindi fractional numbers with the values shown in right by drawing a line between them.

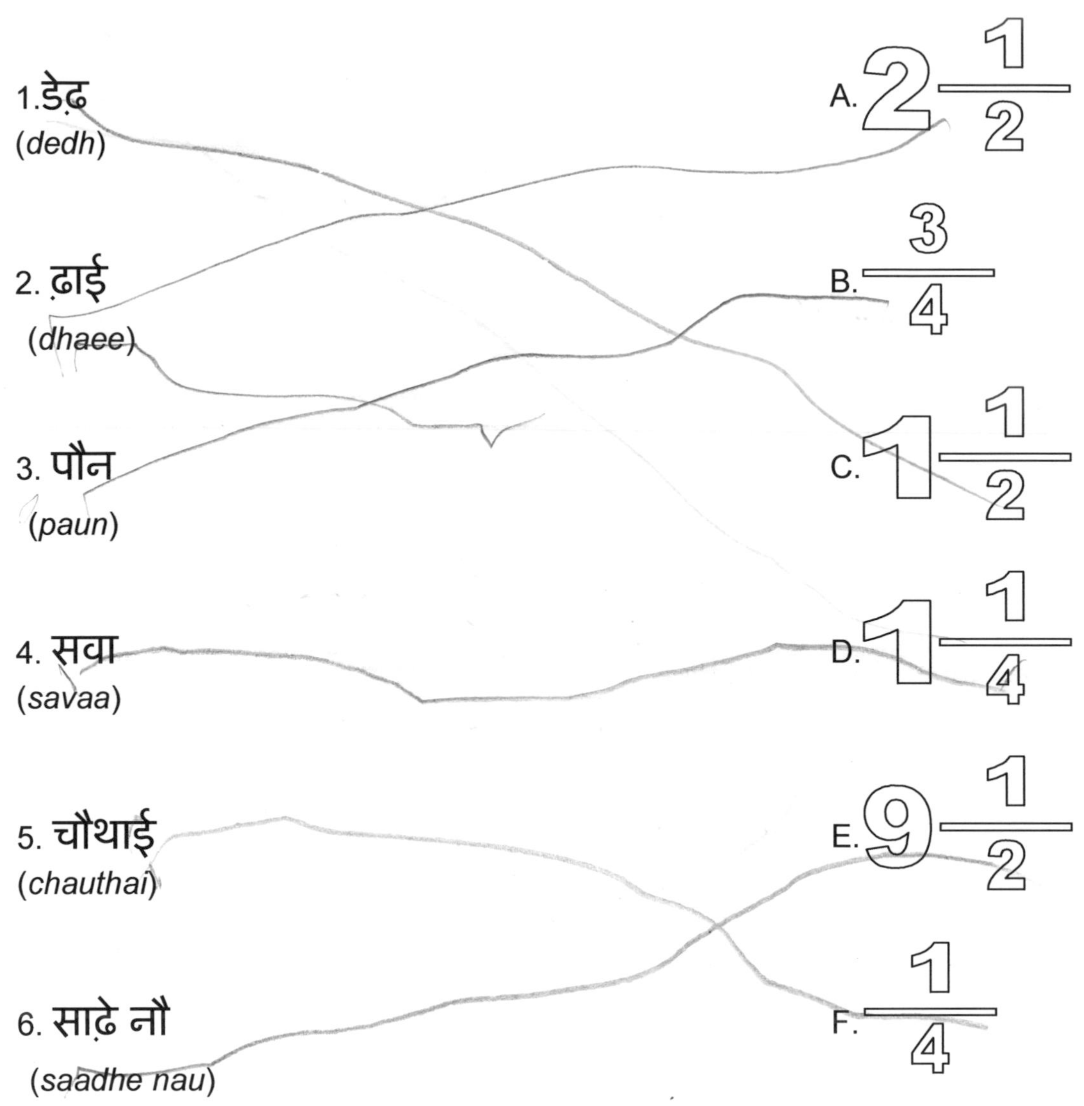

Answers:
Note: सवा means quarter more, पौने means quarter less and साढ़े means half more

1.	C	4.	D
2.	A	5.	F
3.	B	6.	E

Time/समय

Match these words in Hindi with their English equivalent by drawing a line from the Hindi word to the corresponding English word.

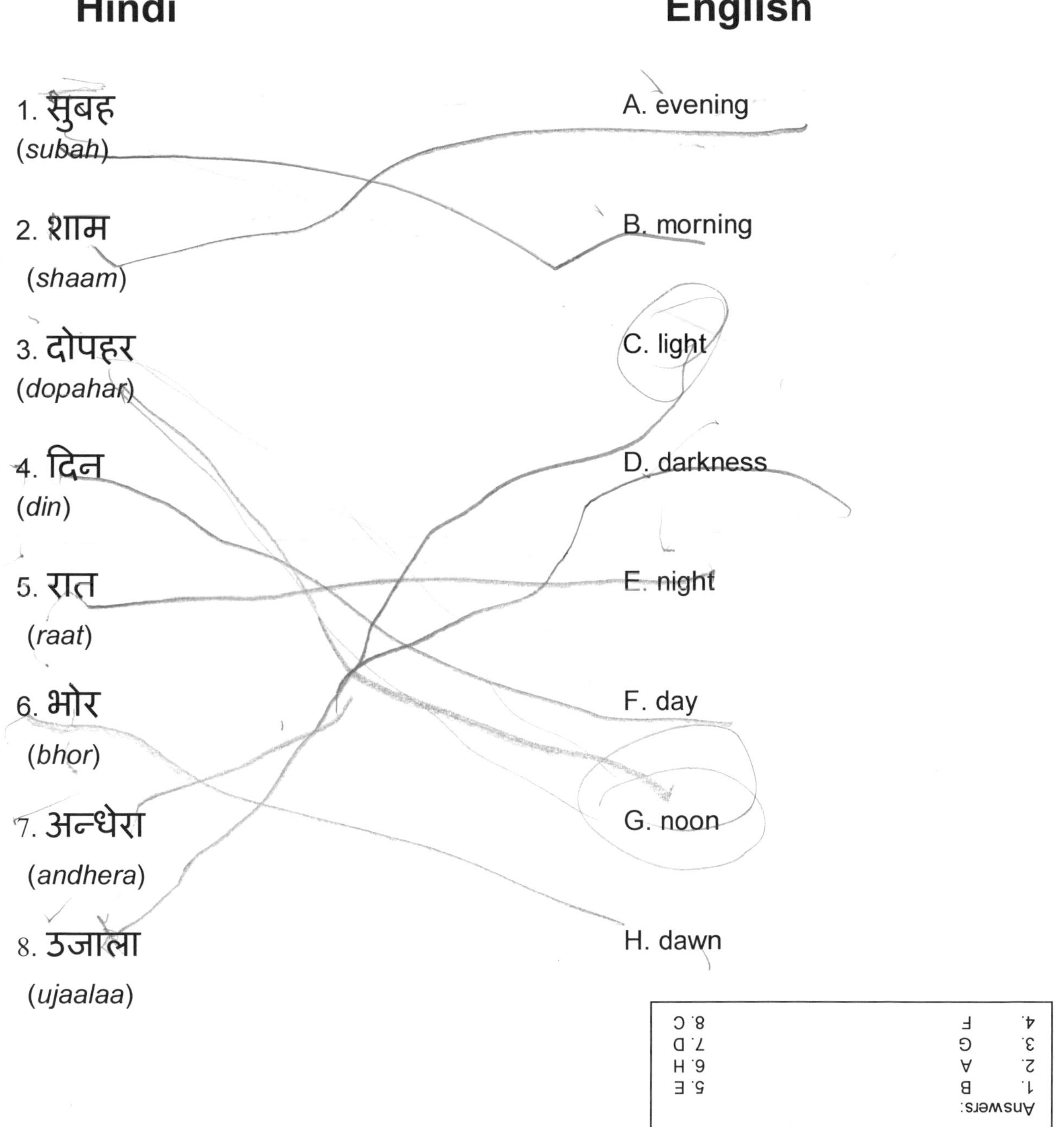

Hindi	English
1. सुबह (*subah*)	A. evening
2. शाम (*shaam*)	B. morning
3. दोपहर (*dopahar*)	C. light
4. दिन (*din*)	D. darkness
5. रात (*raat*)	E. night
6. भोर (*bhor*)	F. day
7. अन्धेरा (*andhera*)	G. noon
8. उजाला (*ujaalaa*)	H. dawn

Answers:
1. B
2. A
3. G
4. F
5. E
6. H
7. D
8. C

Time/समय

Match these words in Hindi with their English equivalent by drawing a line from the Hindi word to its corresponding English word.

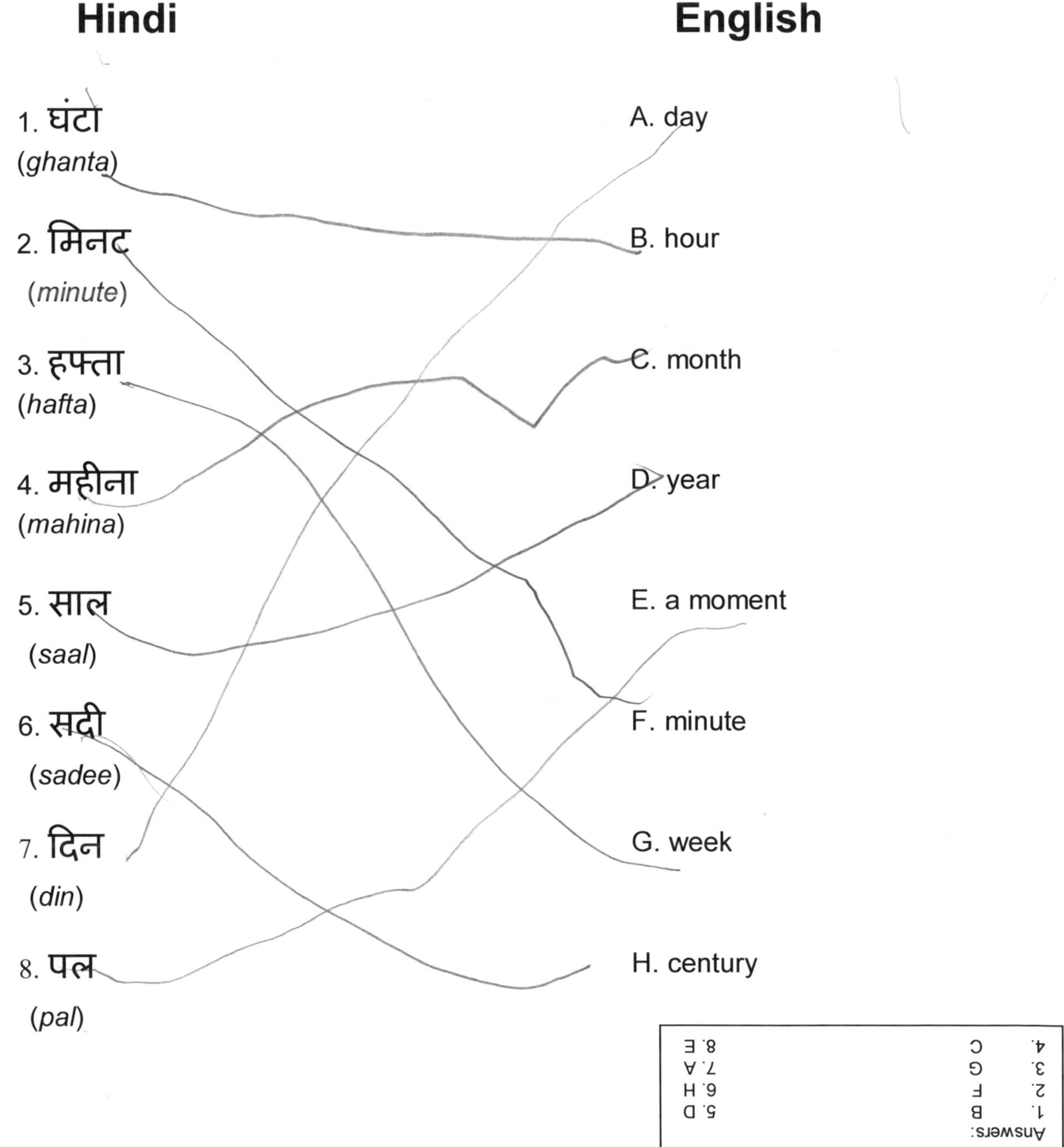

Time/समय

Match the Hindi time with the clock shown on the right by drawing a line between the time and the clock that shows that time.

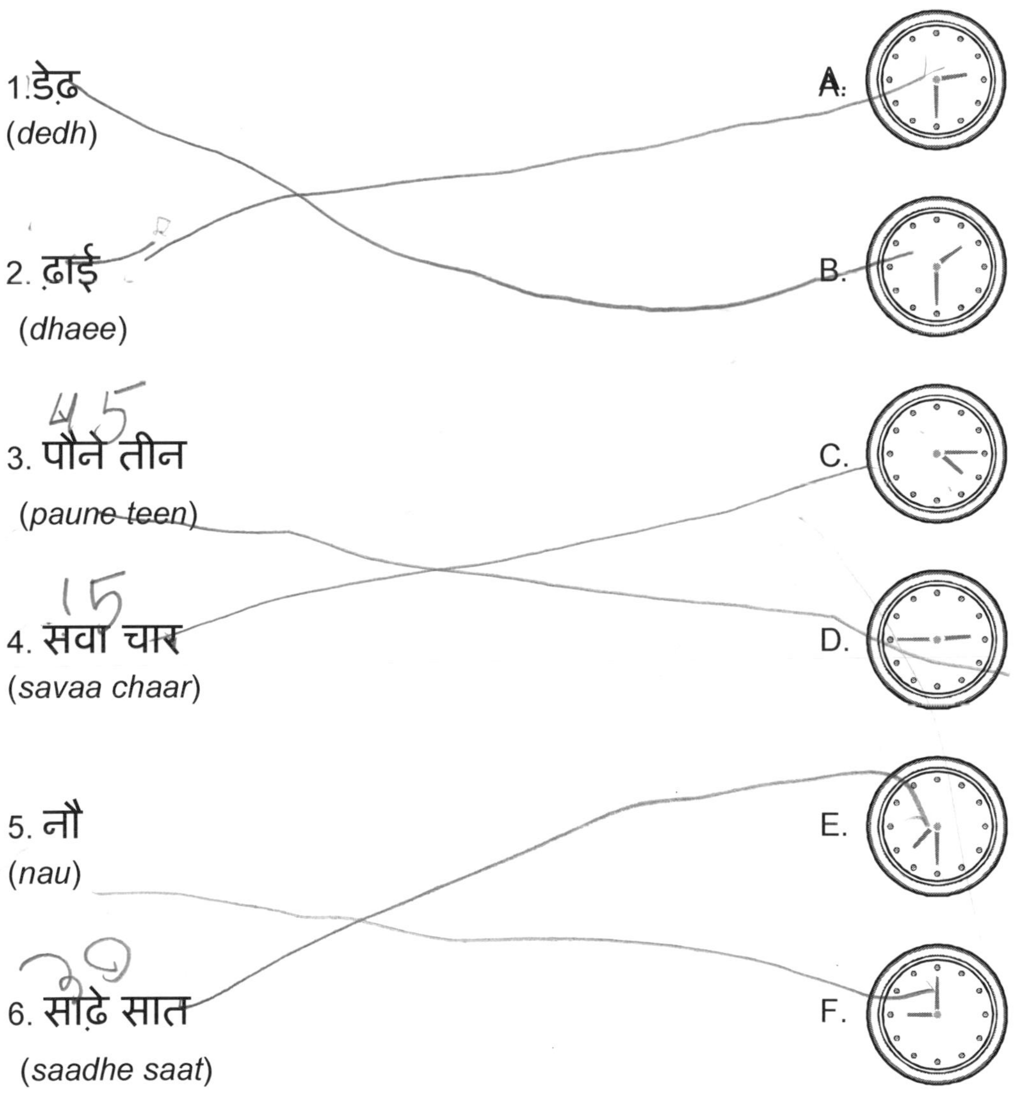

1. डेढ़ (*dedh*)
2. ढाई (*dhaee*)
3. पौने तीन (*paune teen*)
4. सवा चार (*savaa chaar*)
5. नौ (*nau*)
6. साढ़े सात (*saadhe saat*)

Answers:
Note: सवा means quarter past, पौने means quarter before and साढ़े means half past

1. B		4. C
2. A		5. F
3. D		6. E

Time/समय

Match these days of week written in Hindi with their English names by drawing a line between them.

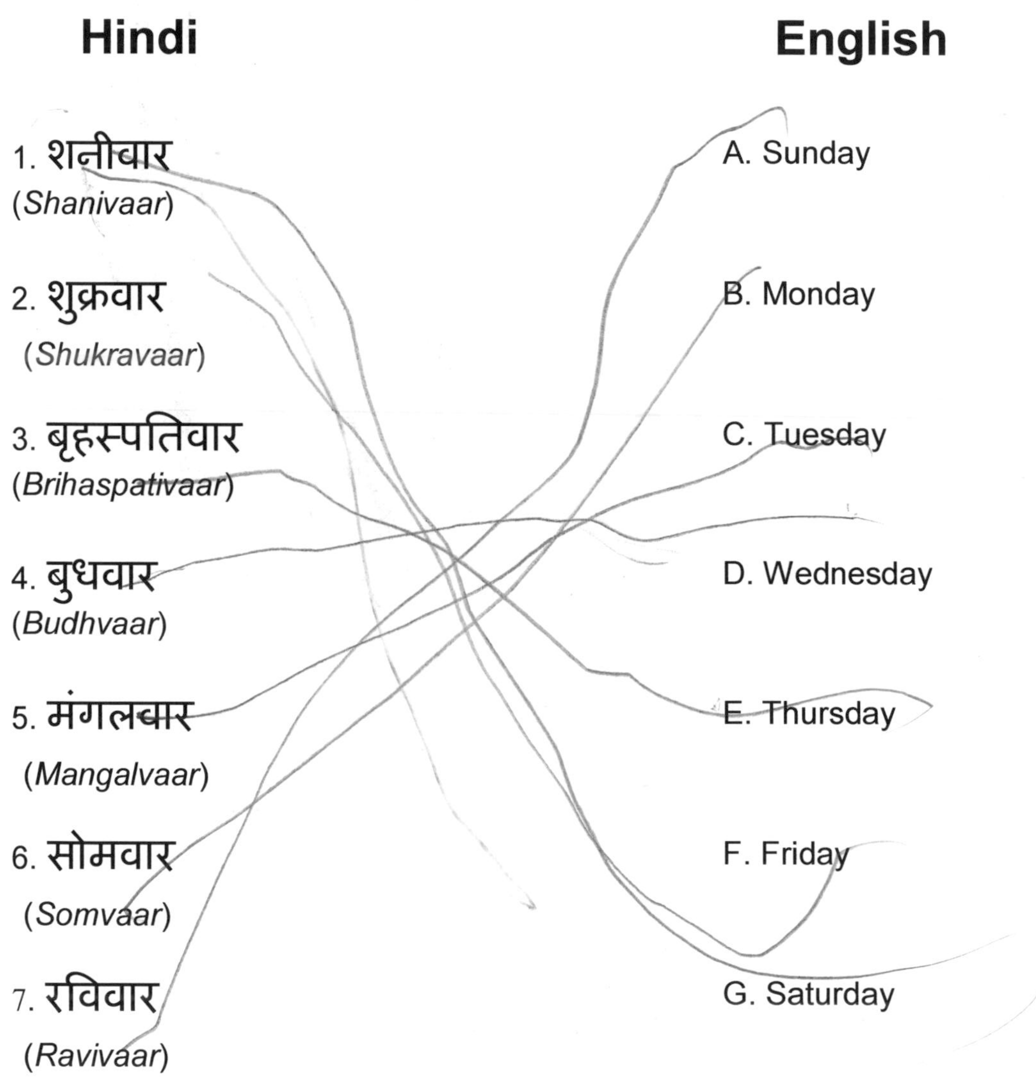

Answers:
1. G
2. F
3. E
4. D
5. C
6. B
7. A

Time/समय

Write down the number of the month (महीना) of the year which corresponds to the month, i.e. 1 for January, 2 for February etc.
Hint: *the months of English calendar are simply written down in Hindi script.*

A. अक्टूबर

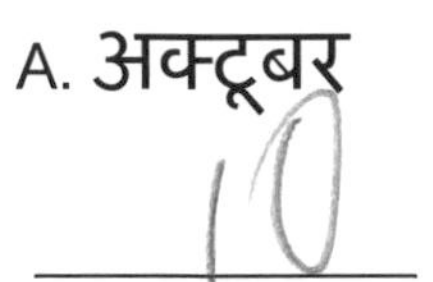

B. अगस्त

C. सितम्बर

9

D. अप्रेल

4

E. दिसम्बर

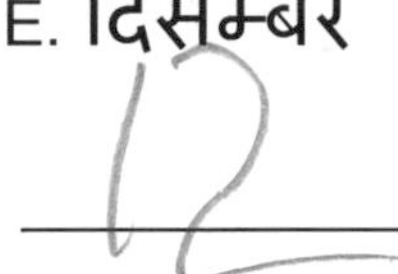

F. नवम्बर

G. मई

5

H. मार्च

I. फरवरी

J. जून

K. जुलाई

7

L. जनवरी

1

Answers:			
A. 10	B. 8	C. 9	D. 4
E. 12	F. 11	G. 5	H. 3
I. 2	J. 6	K. 7	L. 1

Time- Seasons/समय - मौसम

Match the figures below to their seasons given in the middle column.

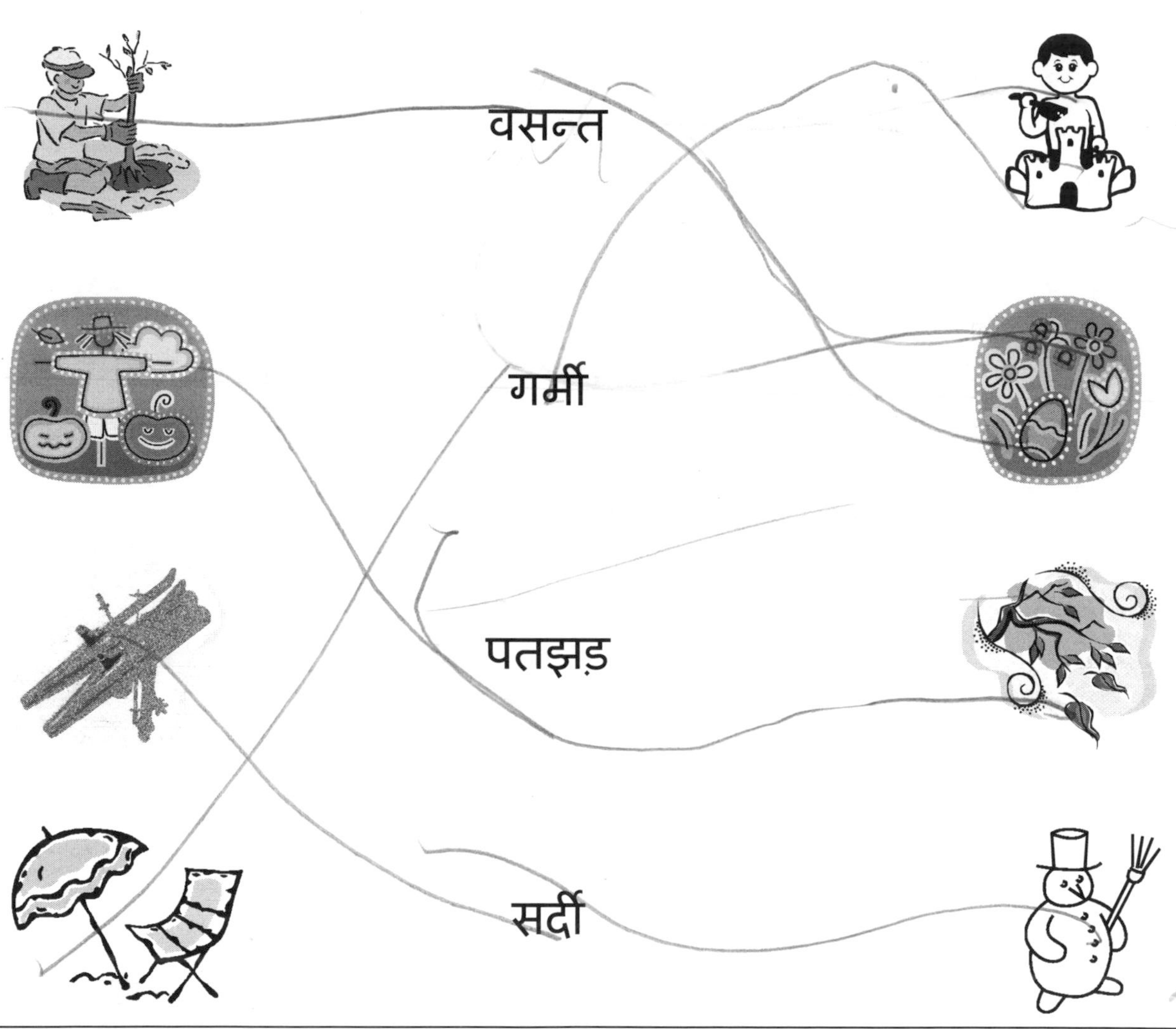

Glossary

वसन्त ....Spring
गर्मी ....Summer
पतझड़......................................Fall
सर्दी ....Winter

Flowers/फूल

The words below list some common flowers. Find each flower in the square and circle them like the first word shown. Each word either goes top to bottom or left to right in the square.

शब्द /Words

गुलाब (gulaab)	rose	नरगिस (nargis)	daffodil
गुलमोहर (gulmohar)	peacock flower	जूही (juhi)	jasmine
चम्पा (champa)	plumeria	रात की रानी (raat ki raani)	night jasmine
चमेली (chameli)	jasmine	केतकी (ketaki)	ketaki
गेंदा (gainda)	marigold	कमल (kamal)	lotus
रजनीगंधा(rajanigandha)	tuberose	पारिजात (parijat)	coral jasmine
गुलदाऊदी (guldaudi)	chrysanthemum	चम्पक (champak)	Arabian jasmine
कनेर (kaner)	oleander	बेली (beli)	jasmine
सूर्यमुखी (suryamukhi)	sunflower	हरसिंगार (harsingar)	coral jasmine
केसर (kesar)	saffron	मोगरा (mogra)	Arabian jasmine

र	ज	नी	गं	धा	क	र	म	ह	गु
पा	रि	जा	ही	गु	ला	ब	च	म्पा	ल
गा	रा	क	म	ल	न	के	मे	बे	दा
बे	त	ने	ट	मो	ह	त	ली	सू	ऊ
गें	की	र	ट	ह	र	की	न	र्य	दी
र्य	रा	मो	ह	र	सिं	गा	र	पा	न
गि	नी	ट	मो	ट	सू	ट	गि	रि	र
ऊ	के	बे	ग	जू	र्य	न	दी	जा	गि
दी	स	ली	रा	ही	मु	ऊ	न	त	स
न	र	गि	स	ट	खी	ह	मे	गें	दा

Fruits/फल

This staircase consists of a fruit on each step. Can you put the Hindi name of the fruit shown on each step?

Fruits

केला (kela) .... bananas
तरबूज(tarbuj)......... watermelon
सेब (seb)............... apple
अंगूर (angur).......... grapes
अनानास(ananas).....pineapple
नीम्बू (nimbu)..........lemon

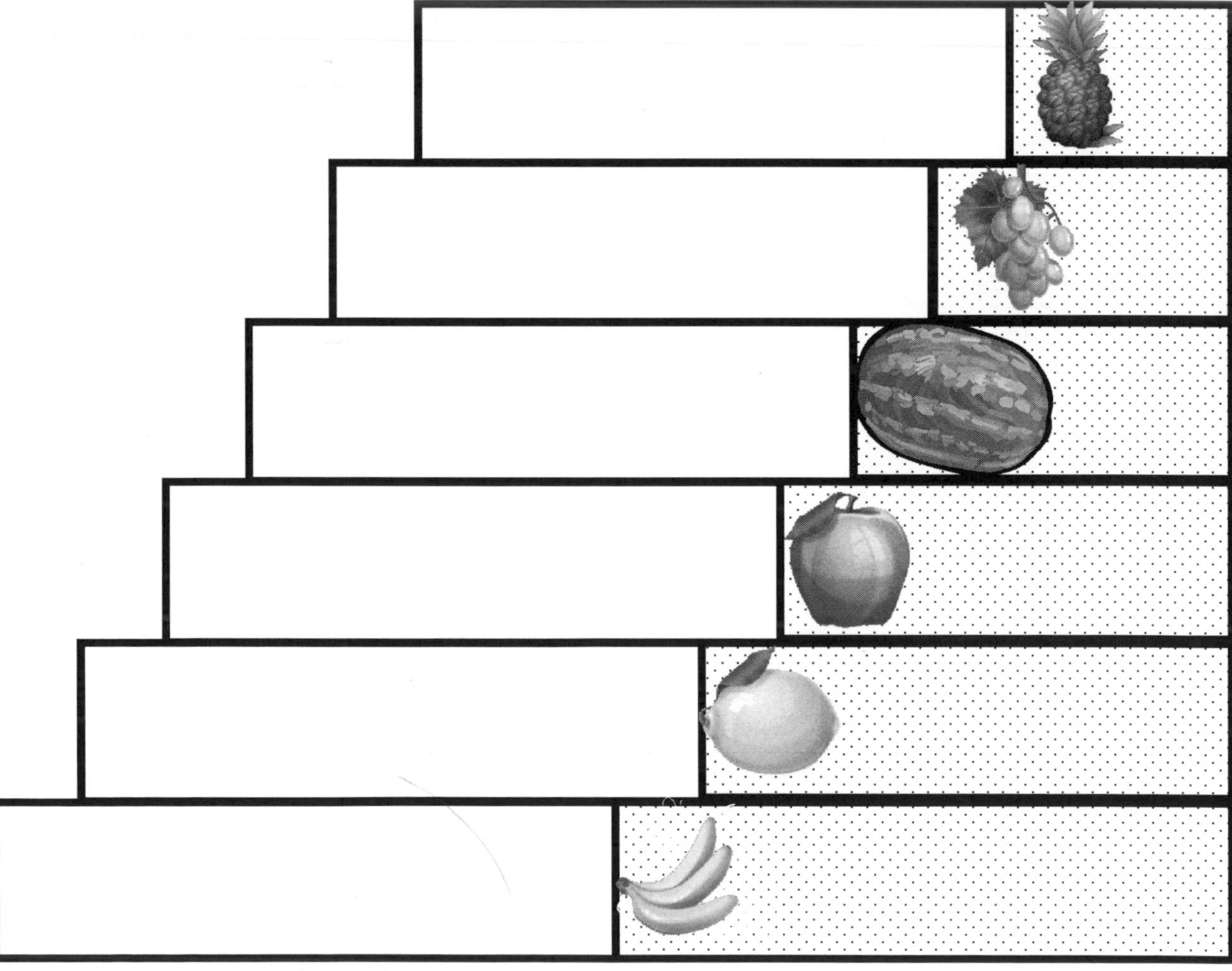

Fruits/फल

Match these words for fruits with their pictures.

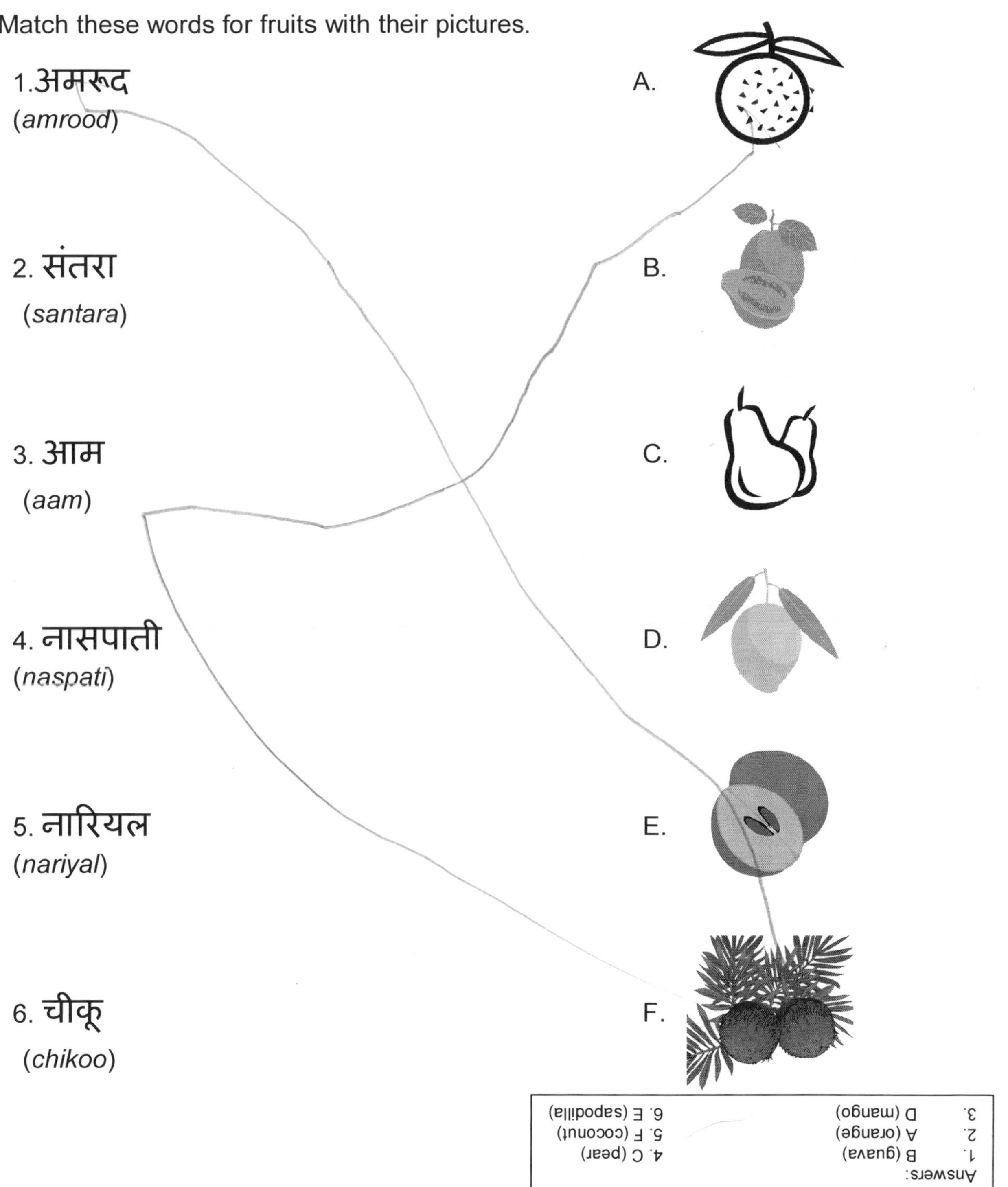

1. अमरूद (*amrood*)
2. संतरा (*santara*)
3. आम (*aam*)
4. नासपाती (*naspati*)
5. नारियल (*nariyal*)
6. चीकू (*chikoo*)

A.
B.
C.
D.
E.
F.

Answers:
1. B (guava)
2. A (orange)
3. D (mango)
4. C (pear)
5. F (coconut)
6. E (sapodilla)

Vegetables/सब्जी

This staircase consists of a vegetable on each step. Can you put the Hindi name of the vegetable shown on each step?

Vegetables
भुट्टा (bhutta) .... corn
मटर(matar)............................peas
चुकन्दर (chukandar)...............beetroot
टमाटर (tamatar)......................tomato
लौकी(lauki)..............................gourd
लहसुन (lahasun).....................garlic

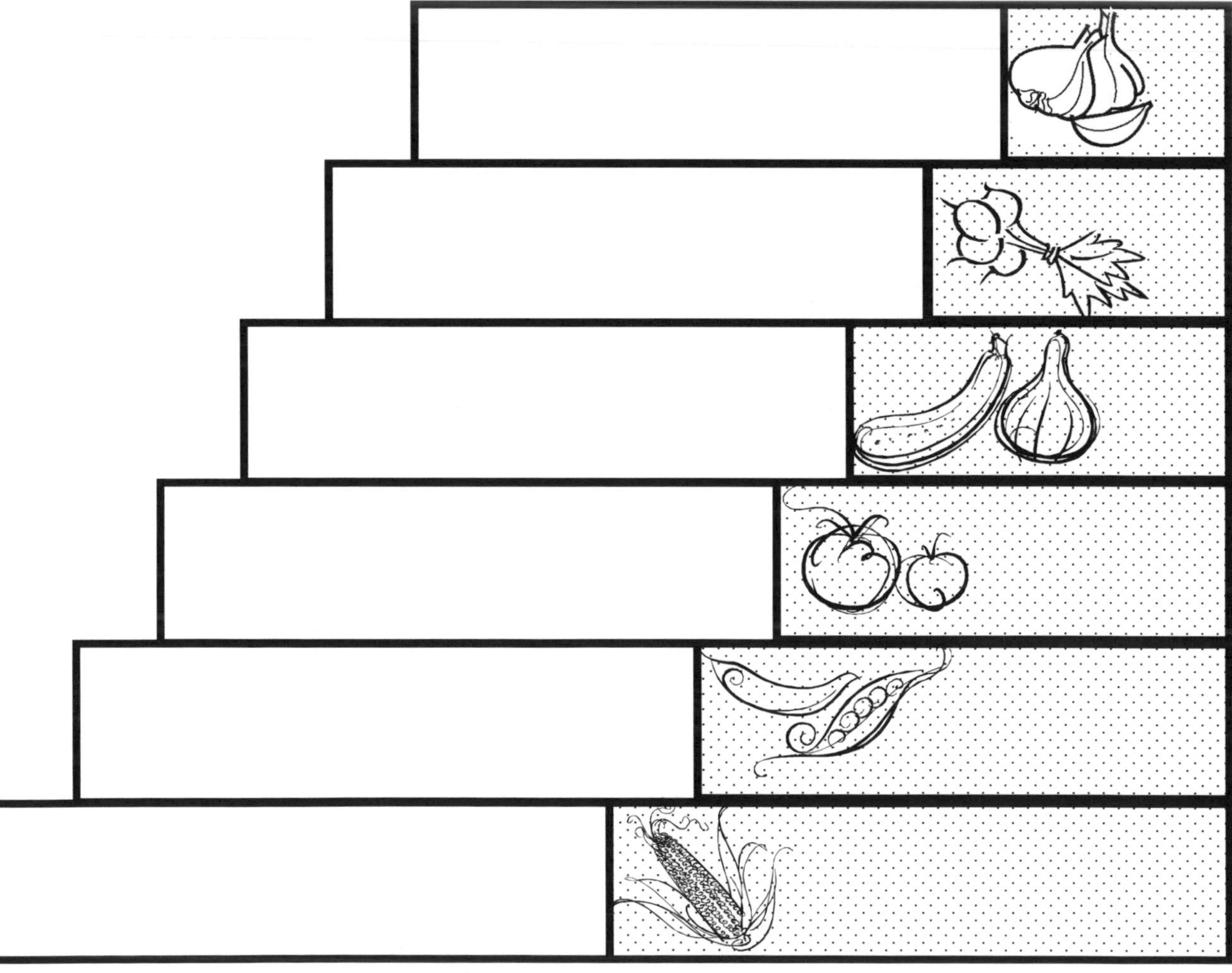

Vegetables/सब्जी

Match these words for vegetables with their pictures.

1.मूली
(*mooli*)

A. 

2. प्याज
(*pyaaj*)

B.

3. मिर्ची
(*mirchi*)

C. 

4. गाजर
(*gaajar*)

D. 

5. बैंगन
(*baingan*)

E. 

6. आलू
(*aaloo*)

F. 

Answers:
1. B (radish)
2. A (onion)
3. D (chilli pepper)
4. C (carrot)
5. F (bringal)
6. E (potato)

Vegetables/सब्जी

Match these words for vegetables with their pictures.

1. तुरई
(*turai*)

2. शलजम
(*shalajam*)

3. खीरा
(*kheera*)

4. शिमला मिर्च
(*shimla mirch*)

5. कद्दू
(*kaddu*)

6. गोभी
(*gobhi*)

A. 

B. 

C.

D.

E.

F.

Answers:
1. B (squash)
2. A (turnip)
3. C (cucumber)
4. E (pepper)
5. F (pumpkin)
6. D (cauliflower)

Relations/रिश्ते

Look at the family tree of Luv below and use that to name the people listed below.

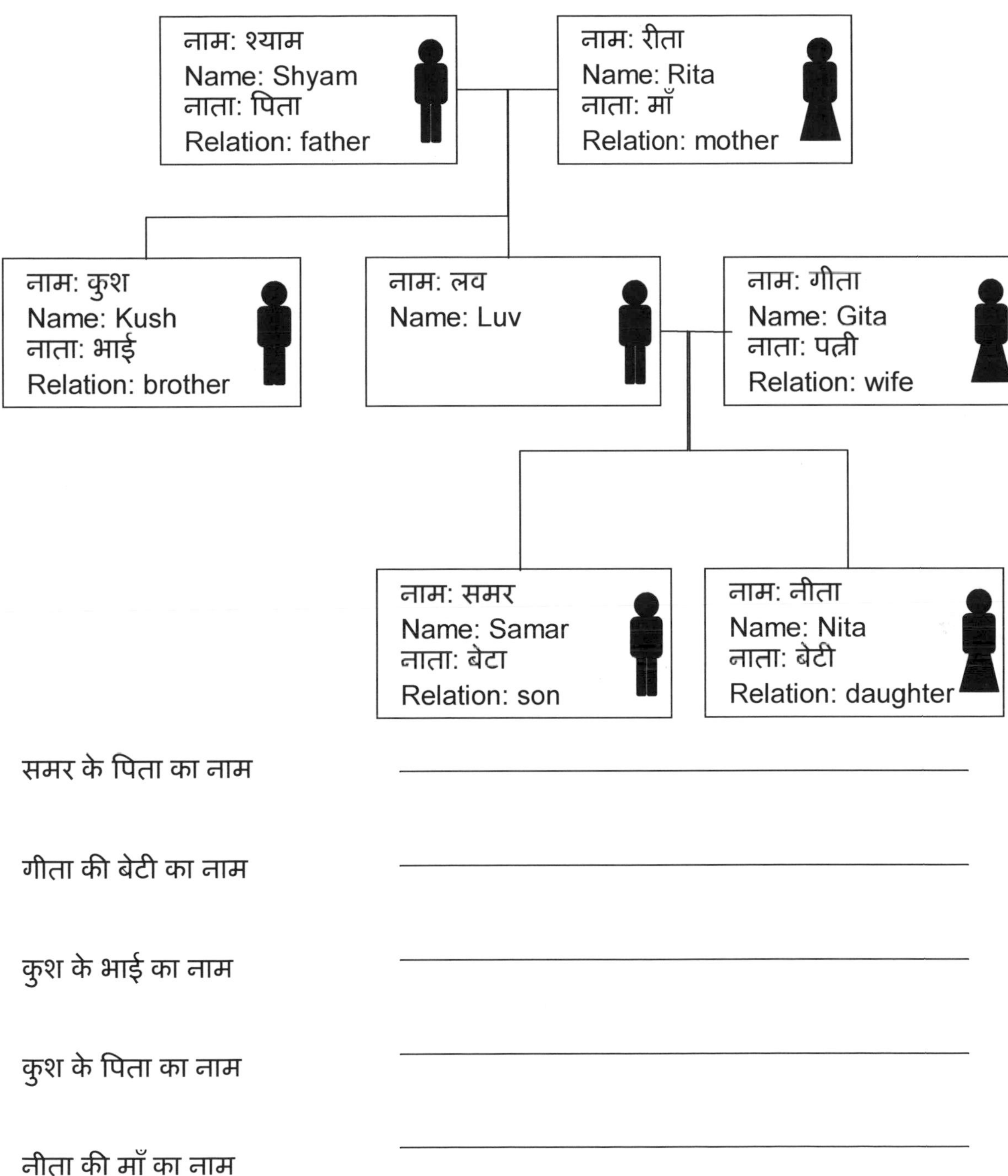

समर के पिता का नाम ______________________

गीता की बेटी का नाम ______________________

कुश के भाई का नाम ______________________

कुश के पिता का नाम ______________________

नीता की माँ का नाम ______________________

Relations/रिश्ते

Match the relation name in the left column with the relation type in second column.

Relation Name	Relation Type
1. दादा (*dada*)	A. माँ का पिता
2. नाना (*nana*)	B. पिता का पिता
3. चाचा (*chacha*)	C. माँ की माँ
4. चाची (*chacha*)	D. पिता की माँ
5. नानी (*nani*)	E. पिता का भाई
6. दादी (*daadi*)	F. भाई का बेटा
7. भतीजा (*bhateeja*)	G. भाई की बेटी
8. भतीजी (*bhateeji*)	H. चाचा की पत्नी

Answers:
1. B
2. A
3. E
4. H
5. C
6. D
7. F
8. G

Relations/रिश्ते

Some relations are reciprocal, e.g. if I am the son of a person, that person is my father. The first column has some relations and the second column the reciprocal relations. Draw a line from the relations to their reciprocal relations in second column.

Relation Name	Reciprocal Relation Name
1. दादा (*dada*)	A. पुत्र (*putra*)
2. मामा (*mama*)	B. नतिनी (*natini*)
3. चाचा (*chacha*)	C. भानजा (*bhanja*)
4. पिता (*pita*)	D. पोता (*pota*)
5. माँ(*ma*)	E. बहन (*bahan*)
6. भाई (*bhai*)	F. बेटी (*beti*)
7. नानी (*nani*)	G. पत्नी (*patni*)
8. पति (*pati*)	H. भतीजा (*bhateeja*)

Answers:

1. D (दादा – paternal grandfather, पोता son of son)
2. C (मामा – mother's borther, भानजा – sister's son)
3. H (चाचा – father's brother, भतीजा – brother's son)
4. A (पिता – father, पुत्र – son)
5. F (माँ – mother, बेटी – daughter)
6. E (भाई – brother, बहन – sister)
7. B (नानी – mother's mother, नतिनी – daughter's daughter)
8. G (पति – husband, पत्नी – wife)

Body Parts/शरीर के अंग

Write the names of the different body parts shown in the figure using the words in the table.

अंगों के नाम

हाथ (haath) …hand
पैर (pair) …   foot
पेट (pet)…   stomach
घुटना (ghutna) knee
कधा (kandha)shoulder
सीना (seena) chest
एड़ी (eydi)…   ankle
सर (sir) …   head

Body Parts/शरीर के अंग

Write the names of the different body parts shown in the figure using the words in the table.

अंगों के नाम	
माथा (matha)	forehead
कान (kaan)	ear
होंठ (honth)...................	lips
नाक (naak)	nose
आँख (aankh)..................	eye
थुड्डी (thodi)...................	chin
गाल (gaal)).....................	cheek
भौं (bhaun))...................	eyebrow
बाल (baal).....................	hair

Body Parts/शरीर के अंग

Match these names of body parts in Hindi with their English equivalent by drawing a line from the Hindi word to the corresponding English one.

Hindi	English
1. जीभ (*jeebh*)	A. teeth
2. दांत (*daant*)	B. tongue
3. दिल (*dil*)	C. blood
4. खून (*khoon*)	D. heart
5. चमड़ी (*chamadi*)	E. finger
6. अंगुली (*anguli*)	F. sole of foot
7. अंगूठा (*angootha*)	G. skin
8. तलवा (*talava*)	H. thumb

Answers:
1. B
2. A
3. D
4. C
5. G
6. E
7. H
8. F

Clothes/कपड़े

Match these words for men's clothes with their pictures.

1. कमीज
(*kameej*)

2. पतलून
(*pataloon*)

3. रुमाल
(*roomaal*)

4. जूता
(*joota*)

5. मोजा
(*moja*)

6. टोपी
(*topi*)

A.

B.

C.

D.

E.

F.

Answers:

1.	B (shirt)	4.F (shoe)
2.	A (trousers)	5. C (socks)
3.	D (handkerchief)	6. E (cap)

Clothes/कपड़े

Match these words for traditional Indian clothes with the letters shown in the pictures.

1. कुरता (*kurta*)
2. पगड़ी (*pagadi*)
3. पजामा (*pajaama*)
4. साड़ी (*saari*)
5. चोली (*choli*)
6. चुनरी (*chunari*)

Answers:

1.	E (shirt)	4.C (sari)
2.	D (turban)	5. B (Blouse)
3.	F (trousers)	6. A

Animals/जानवर

On the lines in the inner wheel, write the numbers from the list below that gives the name of the **wild animal** (जंगली जानवर) shown on the corresponding outer wheel.

सूची (List)		
1. शेर(sher)	5. भेड़िया (bhediya)	9. ऊँट (oont)
2. चीता(cheetah)	6. हाथी (hathi)	10. वनमानुष (vanamanus)
3. बाघ(bagh)	7. बन्दर (bandar)	11.हिरण (hiran)
4. भालू (bhalu)	8. गैंडा(gainda)	12. लोमड़ी (lomadi)

Answers:

1. D (lion)	5.A (wolf)	9. H (came)
2. J (cheetah)	6.B (elephant)	10.K (ape)
3. L (tiger)	7.E (monkey)	11.G (deer)
4. I (bear)	8.F.(rhinoceros)	12.C (fox)

Animals/जानवर

Match these words for **farm animals** with their pictures.

1.गाय
(*gaay*)

A. 

2. बैल
(*bail*)

B. 

3. भेड़
(*bhed*)

C. 

4. मुर्गी
(*murgi*)

D. 

5. सुअर
(*soo-ar*)

E. 

6. घोड़ा
(*ghoda*)

F. 

Answers:

1.	B (cow)	4.F (chicken)
2.	A (bull)	5. C (pig)
3.	D (sheep)	6. E (horse)

Animals/जानवर

Match these animal names in Hindi with their English equivalent by drawing a line from the Hindi word to its corresponding English word.

Hindi	English
1. गदहा (*gadaha*)	A. buffalo
2. गिलहरी (*gilahari*)	B. donkey
3. भैंस (*bhains*)	C. squirrel
4. नेवला (*nevalaa*)	D. fish
5. मछली (*machhalee*)	E. mongoose
6. बकरी (*bakari*)	F. beaver
7. उदबिलाव (*udbilav*)	G. giraffe
8. जिराफ (*giraf*)	H. goat

Answers:
1. B
2. C
3. A
4. E
5. D
6. H
7. F
8. G

Animals/जानवर

On the lines in the inner wheel, write the numbers from the list below that gives the name of the **bird** (चिड़िया) shown on the corresponding outer wheel.

सूची (List)		
1. मोर (mor)	5. कबूतर (kabootar)	9. उल्लू (ullu)
2. गौरैया (goraiya)	6. कठफोड़वा (kathphoravaa)	10. हंस (hans)
3. गिद्ध(giddh)	7. बगुला (bagulaa)	11.कौवा (kauva)
4. बाज (baaj)	8. शुतुरमुर्ग (shuturmurg)	12. बतख (batakh)

Answers:

1. F (peacock)	5.J (pigeon)	9. A (owl)
2. K (sparrow)	6.H (woodpecker)	10.I (swan)
3. D (vulture)	7.G (crane)	11. C (crow)
4. L (eagle)	8. E (ostrich)	12. B (duck)

Animals/जानवर

Match these words for **reptiles** (सरीसृप) with their pictures.

1. मगर (*magar*)
2. साँप (*saanp*)
3. कछुआ (*kachhua*)
4. छिपकली (*chipakali*)
5. गिरगिट (*girgit*)
6. मेढ़क (*mendhak*)

A.

B.

C.

D.

E.

F.

Answers:
1. B (crocodile)
2. F (snake)
3. E (tortoise)
4. A (lizard)
5. C (chamaleon)
6. D (frog)

Animals/जानवर

On the lines in the inner wheel, write the numbers from the list below that gives the name of the **insect** (कीड़ा)shown on the corresponding outer wheel.

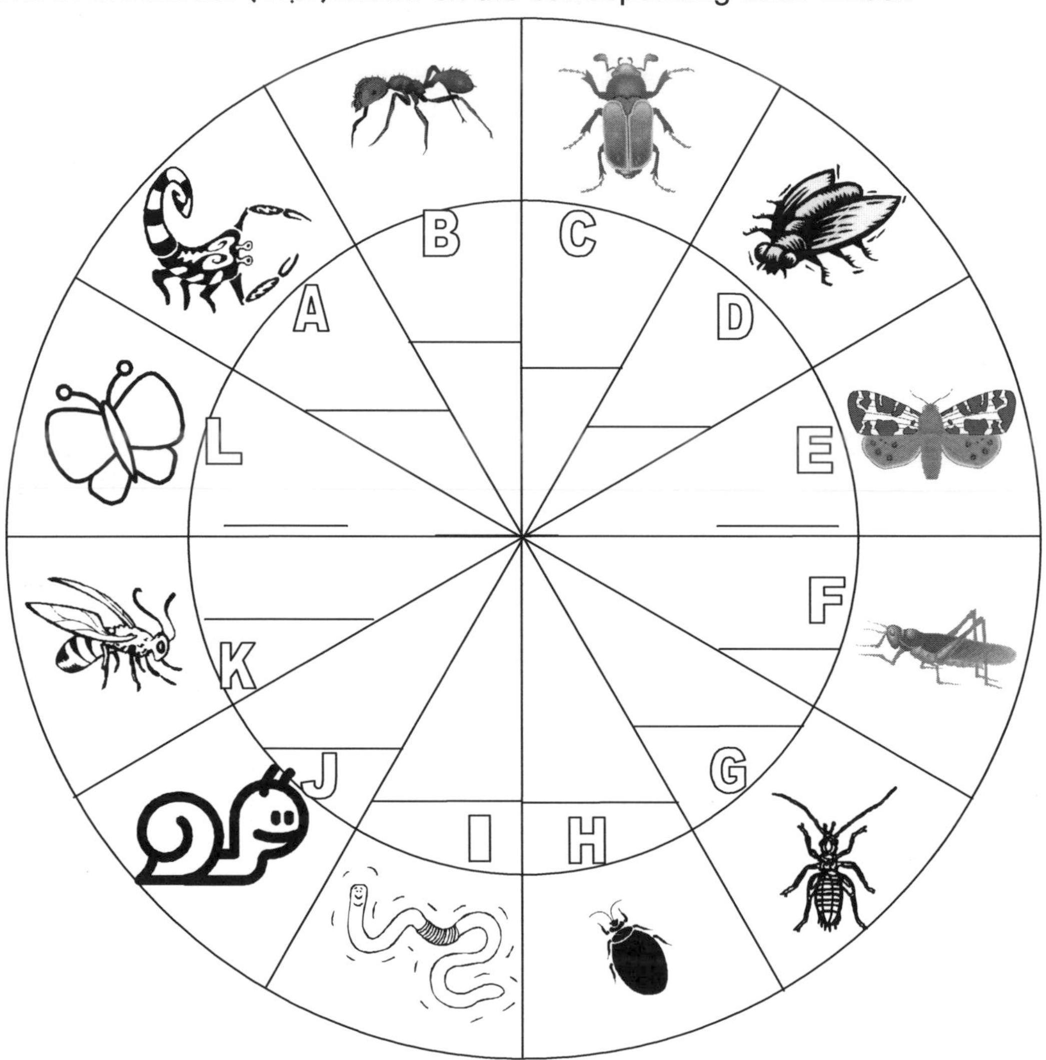

सूची (List)		
1. तितली (titali)	5. मक्खी (makkhi)	9. टिड्डा (tidda)
2. घोंघा (ghongha)	6. पतंगा (patanga)	10. मधुमक्खी (madhumakhi)
3. बिच्छू (bichchu)	7. जूँ (joon)	11.झिंगुर (jhingur)
4. केंचुवा (kenchua)	8. चींटी(chinti)	12. खटमल (khatmal)

Answers:

1. L (butterfly)	5.D (fly)	9. F (locust)
2. J (snail)	6.E (moth)	10. K (honeybee)
3. A (scorpion)	7.G (lice)	11. C (cockroach)
4. I (earthworm)	8. B (ant)	12. H (bedbug)

Animals/जानवर

The words below are hiding in this square. Find them. Circle them like the first word. Each word goes top to bottom or left to right.

शब्द /Words

भालू (bhalu)	bear	नेवला (newala)	mongoose
कुत्ता (kutta)	dog	मछली (machhali)	fish
गाय (gaay)	cow	मगर (mugger)	crocodile
घोड़ा (ghoda)	horse	साँप (saanp)	snake
गदहा (gadaha)	donkey	ऊँट (oont)	camel
बिल्ली(billi)	cat	उल्लू (ullu)	owl
चूहा (chooha)	mouse	गैंडा (gainda)	rhinocerous
शेर (sher)	lion	हिरण (hiran)	deer
हाथी (haathi)	elephant	हंस (hans)	swan
मोर (mor)	peacock	मुर्गी (murgi)	hen

प	रे	द	हि	स	मु	ज	हो	यू	दो
ने	व	ला	पु	भा	लू	दी	ली	कु	जा
व	मु	र्गी	कु	ट	शे	घो	ड़ा	प	चा
ल	गा	य	त्ता	मो	र	ट	चू	रा	र
ह	ट	क	र	गा	ग	द	हा	थी	ट
क	ट	बि	ल्ली	स	ह	ल	सी	टी	की
उ	र	म	छ	ली	ट	ट	ऊँ	ट	को
ल्लू	ल	ग	ट	ट	साँ	प	ट	हं	स
स	च	र	गैं	डा	जा	न	व	र	ह
पि	ता	अ	प	ली	हि	र	ण	क	ल

Animals/जानवर

Match these words for **pet animals** (पालतू जानवर) with their pictures.

1. तोता (*tota*) — A. 

2. बिल्ली (*billi*) — B.

3. कुत्ता (*kutta*) — C. 

4. खरगोश (*kharagosh*) — D. 

5. गिलहरी (*gilahari*) — E. 

6. चूहा (*chooha*) — F. 

Answers:

1.	B (parrot)	4.C (rabbit)
2.	A (cat)	5. F (squirrel)
3.	E (dog)	6. D (mouse)

Colors/रंग

On the lines in the inner wheel, write the numbers from the list below that gives the name of the color written on the corresponding outer wheel.

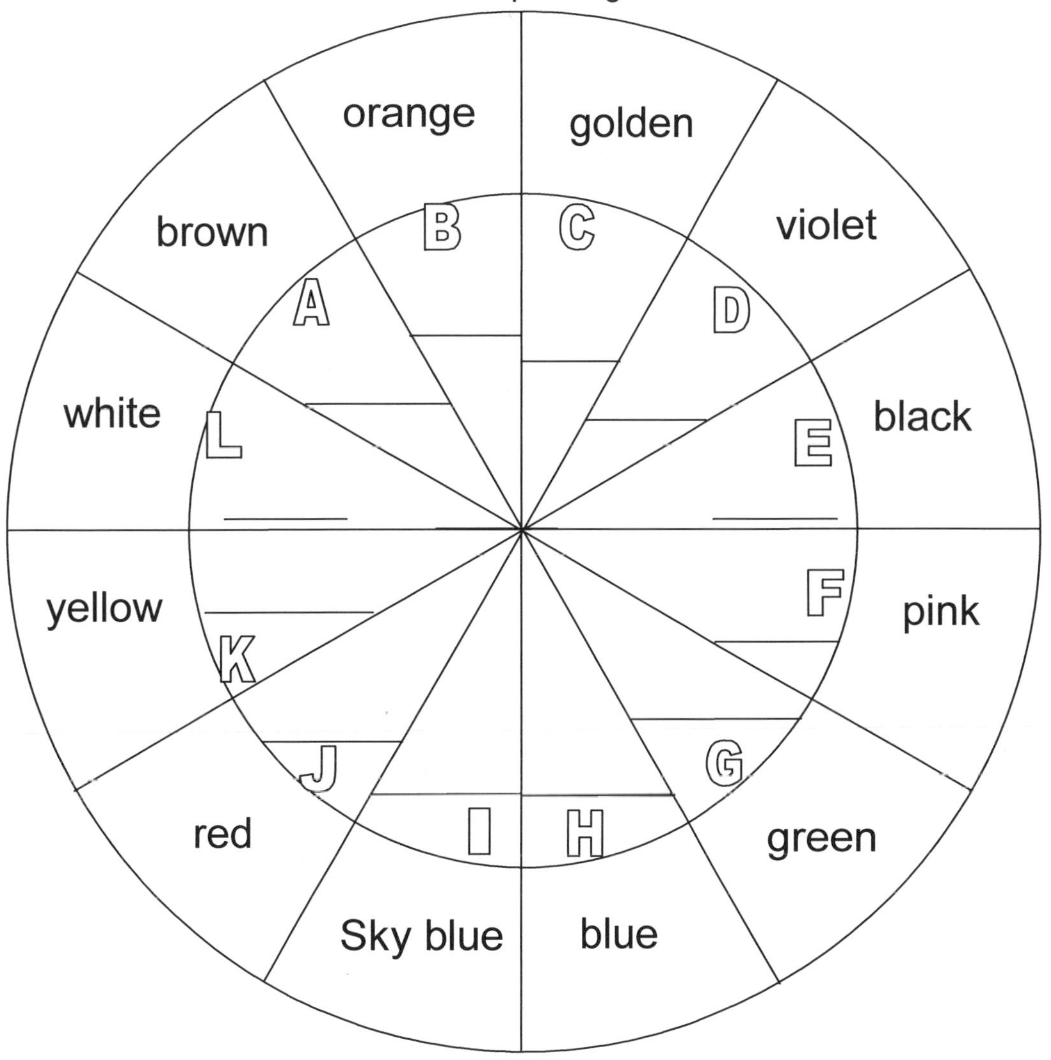

सूची (List)		
1. नीला (neela)	5. लाल (laal)	9. आसमानी (aasmani)
2. पीला (peela)	6. भूरा (bhoora)	10. सुनहरा (sunaharaa)
3. हरा (haraa)	7. सफेद (safed)	11.नारंगी (narangi)
4. गुलाबी (gulaabi)	8. काला (kaala)	12. बैंगनी (baigani)

Answers:

1. H	5.J	9. I
2. K	6.A	10.C
3. G	7.L	11. B
4. F	8. E	12. D

Colors/रंग

The rabbit needs to reach the carrot, but is only allowed to step on stones of black color. The color of each stone is written on it. Find a path for the rabbit to reach the carrot.

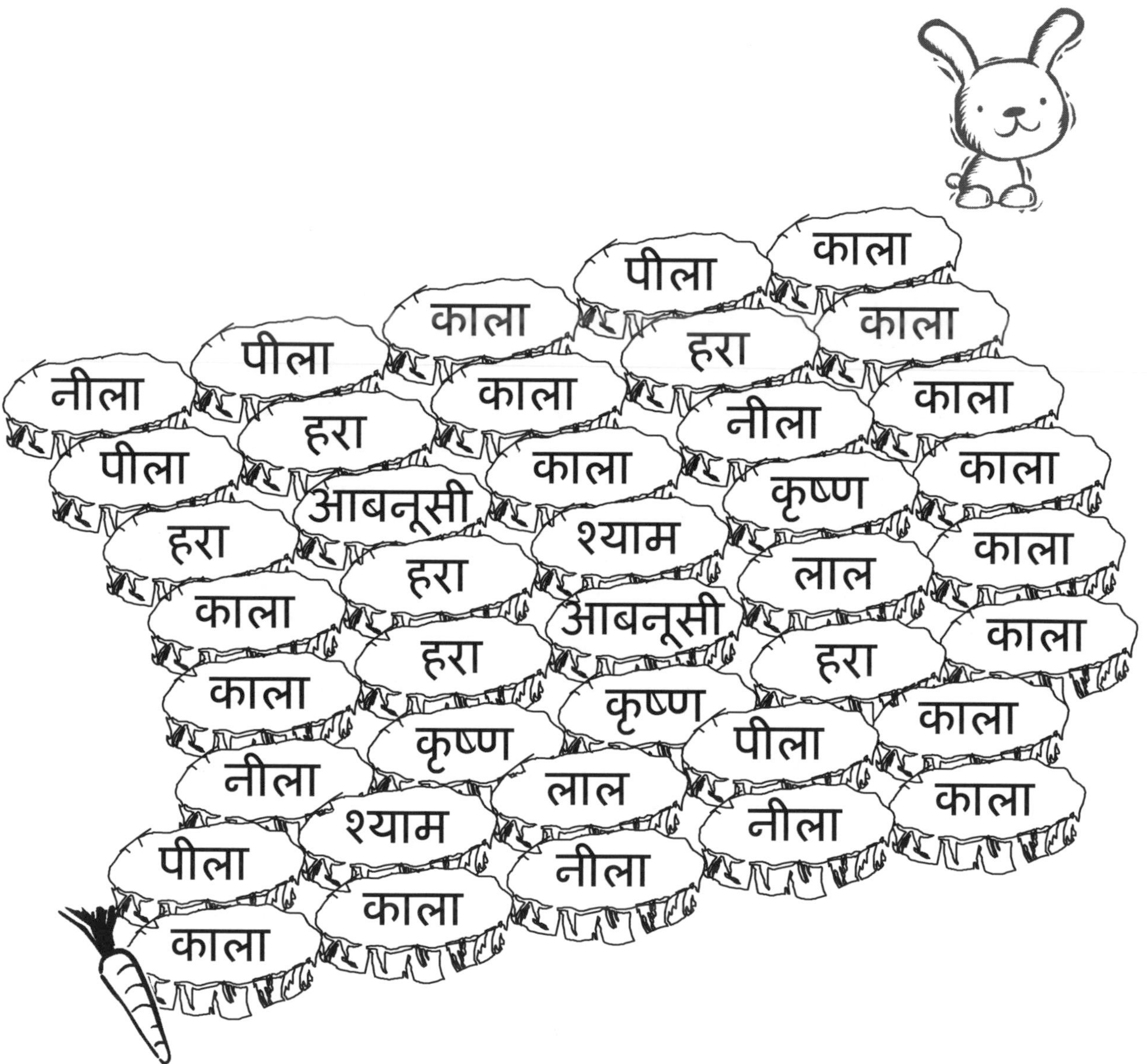

Answer: You can find a path knowing that the words काला, कृष्ण, श्याम, आबनूसी are all synonyms for black.

Nature/प्रकृती

Match these words in Hindi with their English equivalent by drawing a line from the Hindi word to its corresponding English word.

Hindi	English
1. धूप (*dhoop*)	A. rain
2. बारिष (*baarish*)	B. heat
3. गर्मी (*garmi*)	C. sunny
4. सर्दी(*sardi*)	D. cloud
5. बादल(*baadal*)	E. cold
6. बाढ़ (*baadh*)	F. drought
7. इंद्रधनुष (*indra-dhanush*)	G. flood
8. तूफान (*tufaan*)	H. gale
9. आंधी (*aandhi*)	I. cyclone/typhoon
10. सूखा (*sookha*)	J. rainbow

Answers:

1. C	6. G
2. A	7. J
3. B	8. I
4. E	9. H
5. D	10. F

Nature/प्रकृती

Match these words for natural objects with their English equivalent by drawing a line.

Hindi	English
1.पहाड़ (*pahaad*)	A. river
2. नदी (*nadi*)	B. mountain
3. टापू (*taapu*)	C. volcano
4. ज्वालामुखी (*jwalamukhi*)	D. island
5. रेगिस्तान (*registan*)	E. cave
6. गुफा (*gufa*)	F. desert

Answers:
1.B 4.C
2. A 5. F
3. D 6. E

Nature/प्रकृती

Match these words for objects in space (अंतरिक्ष) with their pictures.

1. चांद
(*chand*)

A.

2. सूरज
(*suraj*)

B.

3. शनी
(*shani*)

C.

4. तारा
(*tara*)

D.

5. धूमकेतु
(*dhoomketu*)

E.

6. धरती
(*dharati*)

F.

Answers:

1.	B (moon)	4.C (star)
2.	A (sun)	5. F (comet)
3.	D (Saturn)	6. E (Earth)

Nature/प्रकृती

On the lines in the inner wheel, write the numbers from the list below that gives the name of the plant/plant part shown on the corresponding outer wheel.

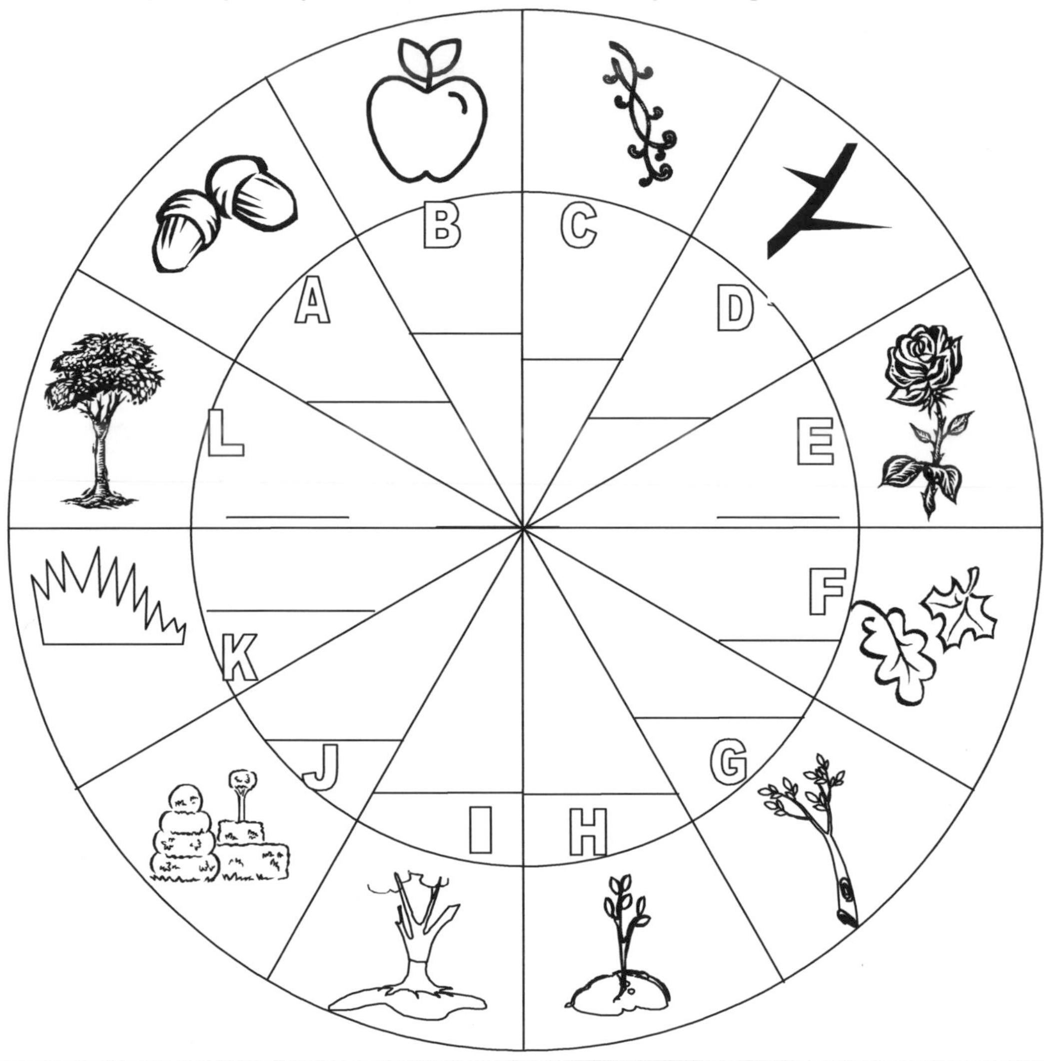

सूची (List)		
1. पेड़ (ped)	5. डाली (daali)	9. बीज (beej)
2. फूल (phool)	6. तना (tanaa)	10. कांटा (kantaa)
3. पत्ता (patta)	7. झाड़ी (jhaari)	11.लता (lataa)
4. पौधा (paudha)	8. घास(ghaas)	12. फल (phal)

Answers:

1. L (tree)	5.G (branch)	9. A (seed)
2. E (flower)	6.I (trunk)	10. D (thorn)
3. F (leaf)	7.J (shrub)	11. C (vine)
4. H (plant)	8. K (grass)	12. B (fruit)

Home/घर

Match these words for bedroom articles with their pictures.

1. बिस्तर
(*bistar*)

A. 

2. पालना
(*paalana*)

B. 

3. तकिया
(*takiya*)

C. 

4. चादर
(*chaadar*)

D. 

5. शीशा
(*sheeshaa*)

E. 

6. कम्बल
(*kambal*)

F. 

Answers:
1. C (bed)
2. A (crib)
3. B (pillow)
4. F (bedsheet)
5. D (mirror)
6. E (blanket)

Home/घर

The words below are hiding in this square. Find them. Circle them like the first word. Each word goes top to bottom or left to right.

शब्द /Words

मेज (mej)	table	पंखा (pankha)	fan
कुरसी (kurashi)	chair	गद्दा (gadda)	mattress
दीवार (deewar)	wall	चादर (chaadar)	bed-sheet
छत (chhat)	roof	गिलाफ (gilaf)	cover
खिड़की (khidaki)	window	चप्पल (chappal)	flip-flops
सीढ़ी(seedhi)	stairs	कपड़ा (kapada)	clothes
कोना (kona)	corner	साबुन (saabun)	soap
पर्दा (parda)	drapes	पानी (paani)	water
कचरा (kacharaa)	garbage	बगीचा (bageechaa)	garden
घड़ी (ghadi)	clock	रसोई (rasoi)	kitchen

कु	ज	ब	कि	कु	द	ग	पं	खा	ट
र	ब	गी	ट	मे	ज	ह	ल	त	खि
सी	म	चा	ह	ख	घ	झ	भ	आ	ड़
स	र	दी	वा	र	ग	सी	ढ़ी	टि	की
घ	ड़ी	चा	द	छ	त	क	का	ग	ट
स	प	ल	न	क	च	रा	ह	द्दा	श
ऊ	ध	र	ट	को	भ	गि	ला	फ	ई
प	र्दा	ङ	व	ना	ब	म	ध	झ	क
ष	ध	सा	बु	न	ङ	र	सो	ई	प
पा	नी	व	च	प्प	ल	ट	ङ	ऊ	ड़ा

Home/घर

Match these words for household articles with their pictures.

1.माचिस (*maachis*)

A. 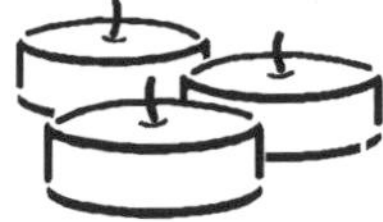

2. मोमबत्ती (*mombatti*)

B. 

3. झाड़ू (*jhaaroo*)

C. 

4. इस्तरी (*istari*)

D. 

5. चाभी (*chaabhi*)

E. 

6. ताला (*taalaa*)

F. 

Answers:

1.	B (matches)	4.C (iron)
2.	A (candles)	5. F (key)
3.	D (broom)	6. E (lock)

Home/घर

On the lines in the inner wheel, write the numbers from the list below that gives the name of the picture shown on the corresponding outer wheel.

सूची (List)		
1. बेलन (belan)	5. थाली (thaali)	9. कांटा (kaanta)
2. कड़ाही (kadahi)	6. प्याला (pyaala)	10. चम्मच (chammach)
3. चूल्हा (choolha)	7. कटोरी (katori)	11.नल (nal)
4. बरतन (bartan)	8. चाकू (chaakoo)	12. कलछुल (kalachhul)

Answers:

1.E (rolling pin)	5.H (plate)	9. G (fork)
2. F (Indian wok)	6.L (cup)	10. A (spoon)
3. K (oven)	7.D (bowl)	11. C (tap)
4. J (pot)	8. I (knife)	12. B (ladle)

Jobs/काम

Match these words for different types of jobs with their pictures.

1.दरजी
(*darjee*)

A. 

2. नाई
(*naee*)

B. 

3. बैरा
(*baira*)

C. 

4. डाक्टर
(*doctor*)

D. 

5. किसान
(*kisaan*)

E. 

6. सिपाही
(*sipaahi*)

F. 

Answers:
1. B (tailor) 4.C (doctor)
2. A (barber) 5. F (farmer)
3. D (waiter) 6. E (policeman)

Jobs/काम

Match these words for different types of jobs with their pictures.

1.पुजारी
(*pujaari*)

A. 

2. डाकिया
(*daakiya*)

B. 

3. दुकानदार
(*dukaandaar*)

C. 

4. बढ़ई
(*badhai*)

D. 

5. वैज्ञानिक
(*vaigyanik*)

E. 

6. गायक
(*gaayak*)

F. 

Answers:

1.	C (priest)	4.E (carpenter)
2.	A (postman)	5. F (scientist)
3.	B (shopkeeper)	6. D (singer)

School/विद्यालय

Match these words in Hindi with their English equivalent by drawing a line from the Hindi word to its corresponding English word.

Hindi	English
1. शिक्षक (*shikshak*)	A. student
2. छात्र (*chhatra*)	B. book
3. किताब (*kitaab*)	C. teacher
4. कलम (*kalam*)	D. uniform
5. पोशाक (*poshak*)	E. pen
6. ईनाम (*eenaam*)	F. paper
7. पढ़ाई (*padhai*)	G. prize
8. कैंची (*kainchi*)	H. glue
9. गोंद (*gond*)	I. scissors
10. कागज (*kaagaj*)	J. studying

Answers:

1. C	6.G
2. A	7. J
3. B	8. I
4. E	9. H
5. D	10. F

School/विद्यालय

Match the Hindi name of subjects you study at school with their English equivalent by drawing a line from the Hindi word to its corresponding English word.

Hindi	English
1. इतिहास (*itihaas*)	A. Science
2. गणित (*ganit*)	B. Languages
3. भूगोल (*bhugol*)	C. Mathematics
4. विज्ञान (*vigyan*)	D. History
5. व्याकरण (*vyakaran*)	E. Geography
6. भाषा (*bhasha*)	F. Physics
7. भौतिकी (*bhautiki*)	G. Arts
8. कला (*kalaa*)	H. Grammar
9. साहित्य (*sahitya*)	I. Music
10. संगीत (*sangeet*)	J. Literature

Answers:
1. D
2. C
3. E
4. A
5. H
6. B
7. F
8. G
9. J
10. I

Farm/खेत

Match these words for farm objects with their pictures.

1.कुआँ
(*kooaan*)

A. 

2. कुदाल
(*kudaal*)

B. 

3. बालटी
(*baalti*)

C. 

4. फसल
(*fasal*)

D. 

5. भूसा
(*bhoosaa*)

E. 

6. बैल
(*bayl*)

F. 

Answers:

1.	B (well)	4.F (crop)	
2.	C (spade)	5. D (hay)	
3.	A (bucket)	6. E (oxen)	

Town/शहर

Match these words for things you see in a city with their pictures.

1.सड़क
(*sadak*)

2. स्कूल
(*school*)

3. चौराहा
(*chauraha*)

4. पुल
(*pul*)

5. दुकान
(*dukaan*)

6. इमारत
(*imaarat*)

A.

B.

C.

D.

E.

F.

Answers:
1. D (road)
2. E (school)
3. A (intersection)
4. C (bridge)
5. F (shop)
6. B (building)

Wealth/धन

This staircase consists of a money-related objecton each step. Can you put the Hindi name of the object shown on each step?

Vegetables

रुपया (rupaya) ....cash/notes

पैसा(paisa)...............................coins

हीरा (heera)..........................diamond

तिजोरी (tijori)..........................safe

बटुआ (batua)..........................wallet

खजाना (khajana)....................treasure

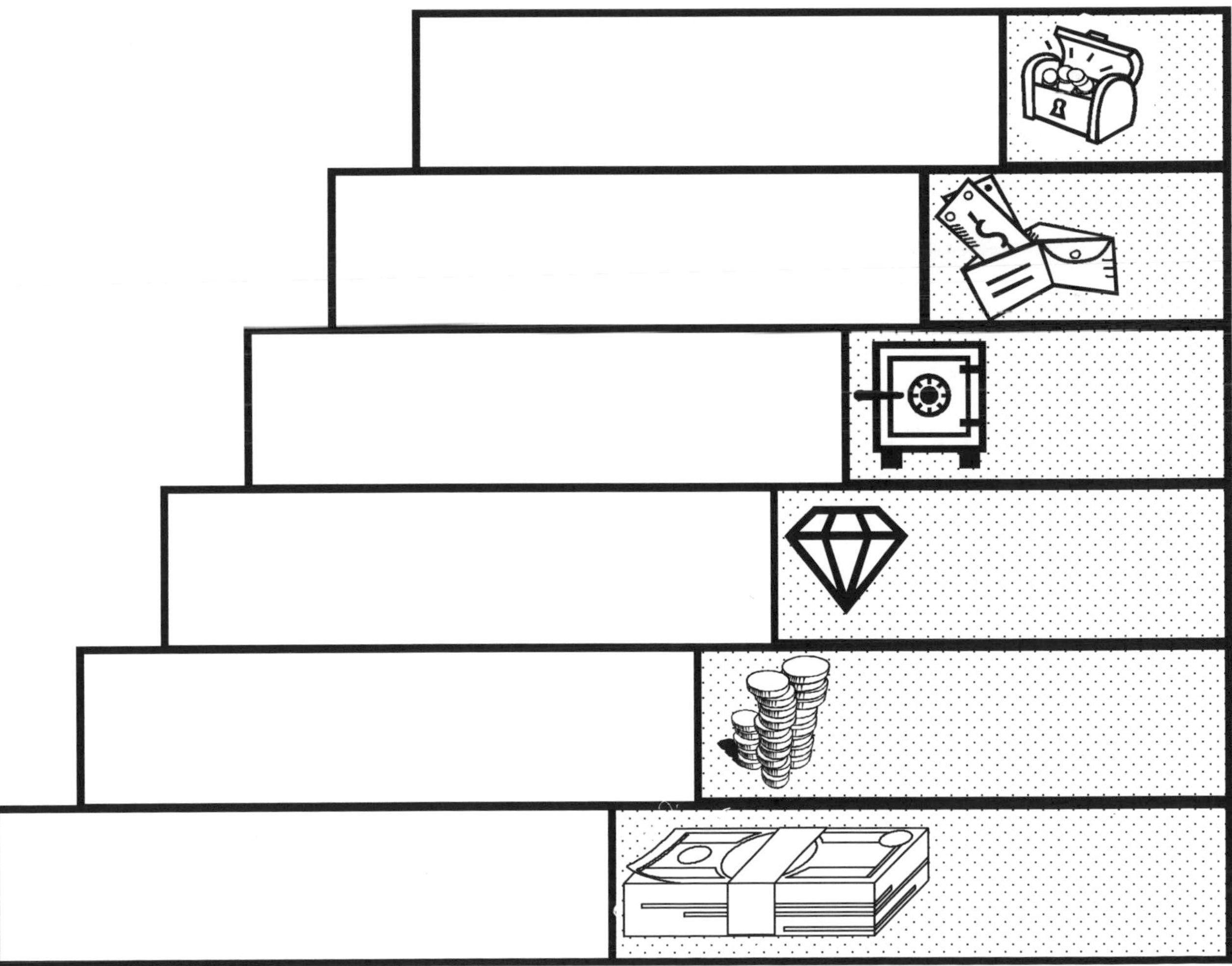

Wealth/धन

Match these words for gemstones in Hindi with their English equivalent by drawing a line from the Hindi word to its corresponding English word.

Hindi	English
1. हीरा (*heera*)	A. coral
2. पन्ना (*panna*)	B. ruby
3. मोती (*moti*)	C. garnet
4. नीलम (*neelam*)	D. diamond
5. पुखराज (pukhraj)	E. emerald
6. मूंगा (*moonga*)	F. pearl
7. माणिक (*manak*)	G. sapphire
8. गोमेद (*gomed*)	H. topaz

Answers:
1. D
2. E
3. F
4. G
5. H
6. A
7. B
8. C

Wealth/धन

Match these words for different pieces of jewelry (गहने) with their pictures.

1.अंगूठी
(*angoothi*)

A. 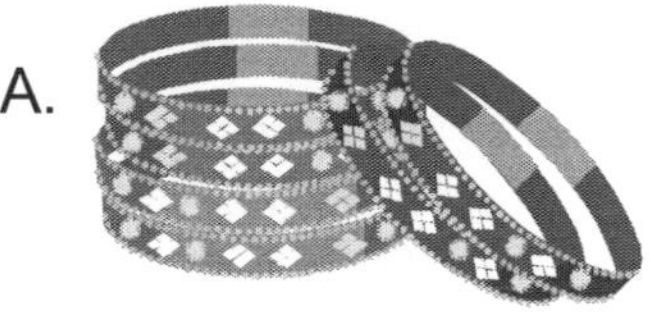

2. हार
(*haar*)

B. 

3. चूड़ी
(*choodi*)

C. 

4. बिंदी
(*bindi*)

D. 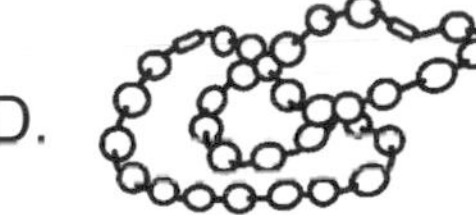

5. बाली
(*baali*)

E. 

6. पायल
(*paayal*)

F. 

Answers:
1. E (ring) 4.B (bindi)
2. F (necklace) 5. C (ear-rings)
3. A (bracelet) 6. D (anklet)

Religion/धर्म

Match these words in Hindi with their English equivalent by drawing a line from the Hindi word to its corresponding English word.

Hindi	English
1. इसाई (*Isai*)	A. Muslim
2. यहूदी (*yahoodi*)	B. Christian
3. गुरुद्वारा (*gurudwara*)	C. Hindu
4. हिन्दू (*hindu*)	D. Sikh temple
5. पूजा(*pooja*)	E. temple
6. मन्दिर (*mandir*)	F. prayer
7. मुसलमान (*musalmaan*)	G. Jew
8. मस्जिद (*masjid*)	H. Sikh
9. सिख (*sikh*)	I. church
10. गिरजाघर (*girjaaghar*)	J. mosque

Answers:
1. B
2. G
3. D
4. C
5. F
6.E
7. A
8. J
9. H
10. I

Religion/धर्म

Match these names for different gods with their pictures.

1. शंकर (*Shankar*) — A. 

2. कृष्ण (*Krishna*) — B.

3. राम (*Raam*) — C. 

4. लक्ष्मी (*Laxmi*) — D. 

5. गणेश (*Ganesh*) — E. 

6. दुर्गा (*Durga*) — F. 

Answers:
1. B
2. A
3. D
4. E
5. F
6. C

Religion/धर्म

The words below related to religious rituals are hiding in this square. Find them. Circle them like the first word. Each word goes top to bottom or left to right.

शब्द /Words

पूजा (pooja)	prayer	अग्नि (agni)	fire
फूल (phool)	flowers	कीर्तन (kirtan)	prayer music
तिलक (tilak)	forehead mark	भजन (bhajan)	prayer song
आरती (aarati)	prayer with fire	शंख (shankh)	conch
कथा (katha)	story	थाली (thal)	plate
प्रसाद(prasad)	blessed food	पुजारी (pujari)	priest
चढ़ावा (chadava)	offering	चंदन (chandan)	sandalwood
व्रत (vrat)	fasting	अक्षत (akshat)	prayer rice
आहुती (aahuti)	offering to fire	दक्षिणा (dakshina)	money to priest
यज्ञ (yagya)	fire ritual	मुहूर्त (muhurt)	auspicious time

य	हु	ब	य	ल	पु	अ	व्र	हु	ब
क्ष	ति	ट	ग्नि	पू	जा	क्ष	ख	ब	ग
फू	ल	ख	ङ	ख	री	ल	क	य	ज्ञ
ट	क	द	क्षि	णा	ट	क	था	ग्नि	त
हु	आ	र	ती	ख	प्र	त	शं	ल	ख
अ	क्ष	त	ङ	घ	सा	ट	ख	क	ग्नि
च	ढ़ा	वा	ख	चं	द	न	र्त	अ	त
प	त	की	र	क्षि	हू	था	ट	ग्नी	ट
र्त	म	र्त	मु	ट	मु	ली	न	च	हु
भ	ज	न	क्ष	मु	हु	भ	मु	हु	र्त

Food/भोजन

On the lines in the inner wheel, write the numbers from the list below that gives the name of the picture shown on the corresponding outer wheel.

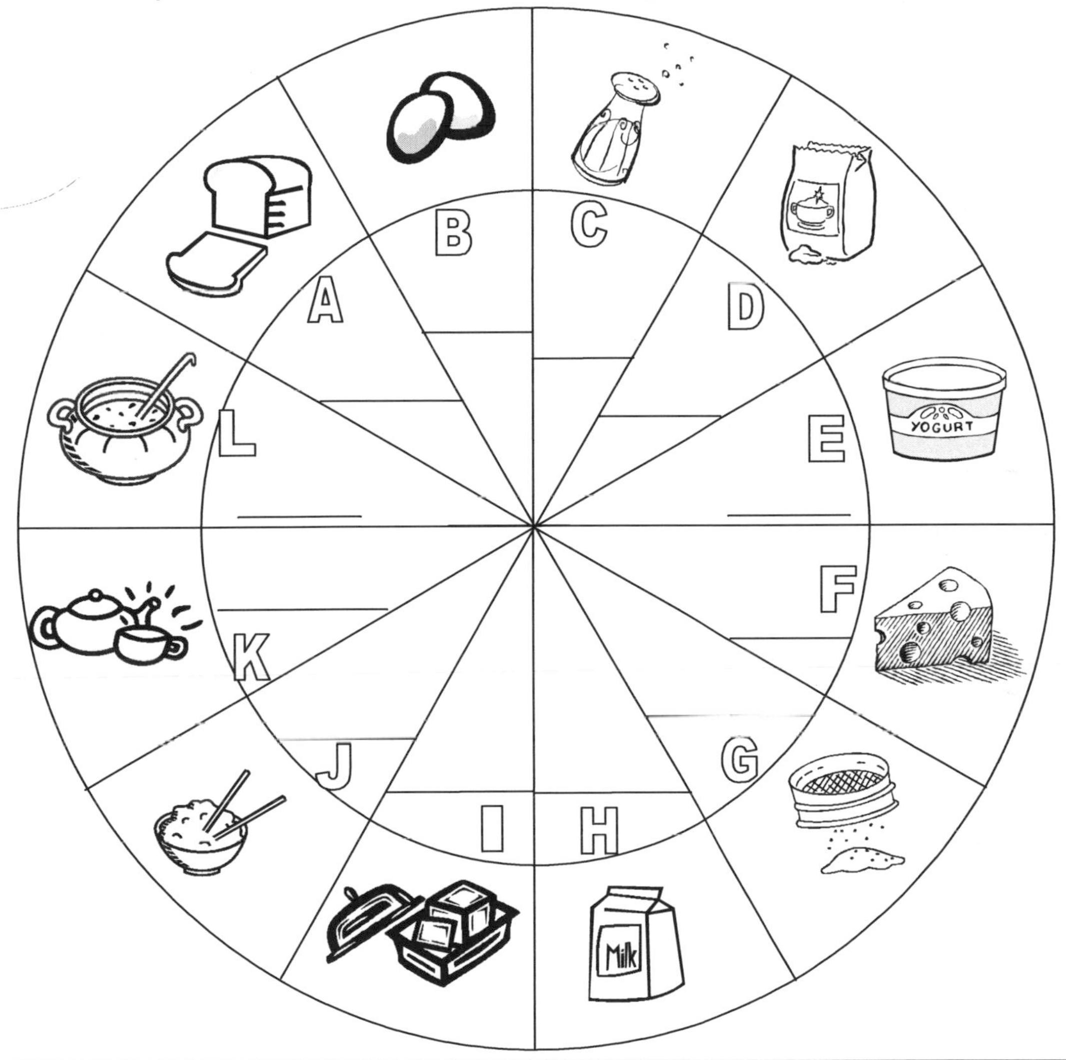

सूची (List)		
1. पावरोटी (paavroti)	5. पनीर (paneer)	9. चाय (chaay)
2. आटा (aataa)	6. चावल (chaawal)	10. नमक (namak)
3. दूध (doodh)	7. दाल (daal)	11.अंडा (andaa)
4. मक्खन (makkhan)	8. दही (dahi)	12. चीनी (cheeni)

Answers:

1.A (bread)	4.I (butter)	7. L (pulses)	10. C (salt)
2. G (flour)	5.F (cheese)	8 E (yougurt)	11. B (egg)
3. H (milk)	6.J (rice)	9. K (tea)	12. D (sugar)

Food/भोजन

Match the names for the different foods with their pictures.

1.मछली झोल
(*machhali jhol*)

A. 

2. जलेबी
(*jalebi*)

B. 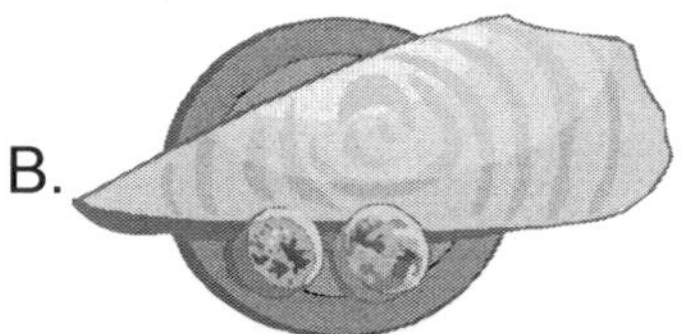

3. डोसा
(*dosa*)

C. 

4. छोला भटूरा
(*chhola - bhatoora*)

D. 

5. ढोकला
(*dhokala*)

E. 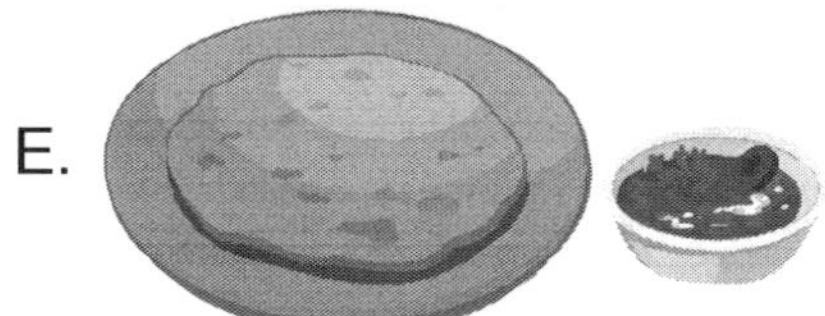

6. रोटी सब्जी
(*roti-sabji*)

F. 

Answers:
1. D 4.C
2. A 5.F
3. B 6.E

Food/भोजन

The rabbit needs to reach the carrot, but is only allowed to step on stones that are marked with names of sweet foods. Find a *sweet* path for the rabbit to reach the carrot.

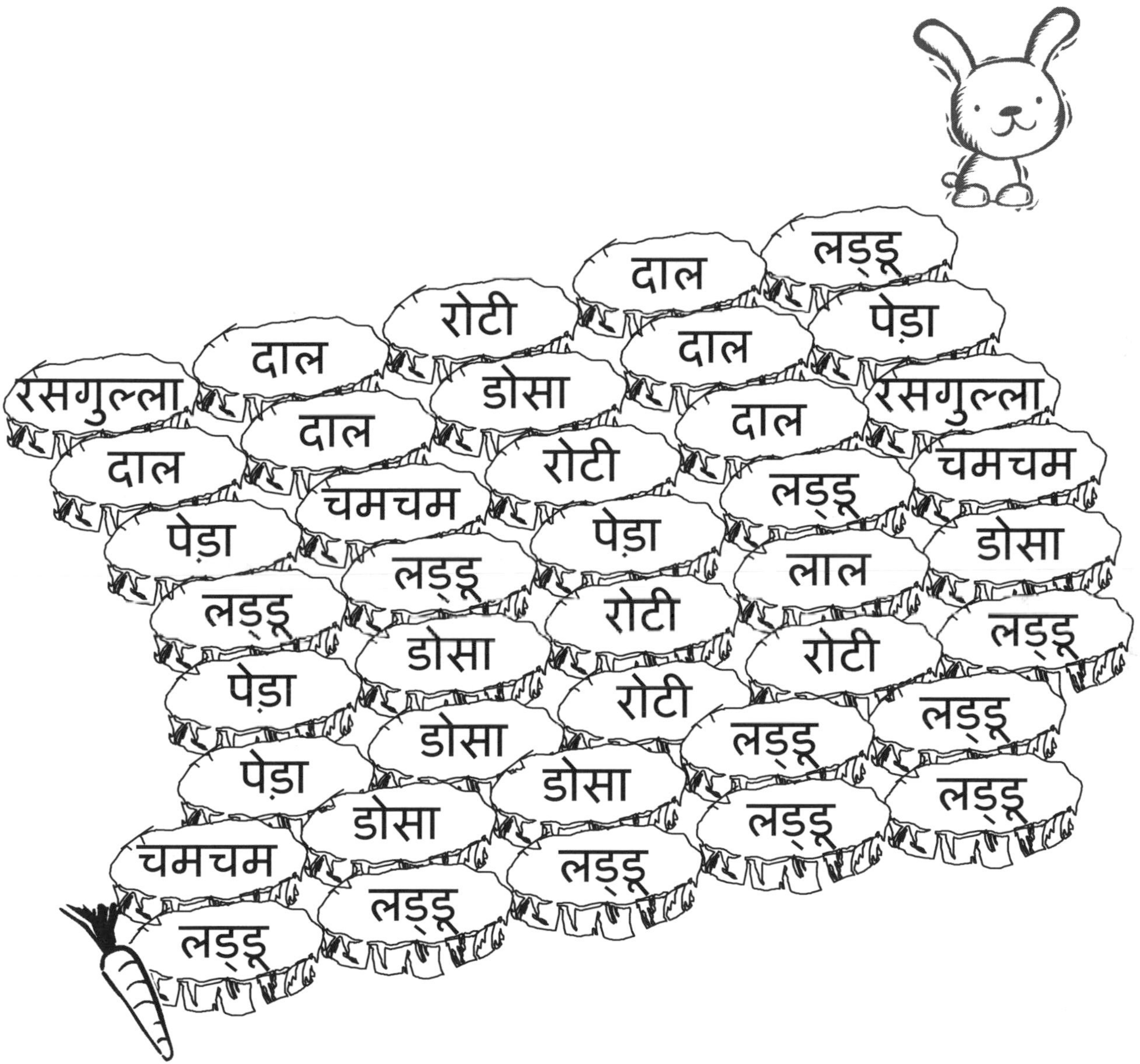

Answer: You can find a path knowing that the words लड्डू, चमचम, पेड़ा, रसगुल्ला are all sweetmeats, and using stones marked with them.

Travel/सफर

Match these names for the different modes of travel with their pictures.

1.साइकल
(*cycle*)

A. 

2. रेलगाड़ी
(*rail-gaadi*)

B. 

3. स्कूटर
(*scooter*)

C. 

4. बस
(*bus*)

D. 

5. कार
(*car*)

E. 

6. वायुयान
(*vayu yan*)

F. 

Answers:
1. B
2. C
3. A
4. D
5. F
6. E

Health/सेहत

Match these words in Hindi with their English equivalent by drawing a line from the Hindi word to its corresponding English word.

Hindi	English
1. सर्दी (*sardi*)	A. headache
2. खान्सी (*khaansi*)	B. cold
3. चोट (*chot*)	C. cough
4. घाव (*ghaav*)	D. bruise
5. बुखार(*bukhar*)	E. wound
6. हिचकी (*hichaki*)	F. fever
7. बीमारी (*bimaari*)	G. hiccups
8. खुजली (*khujali*)	H. illness
9. उलटी (*ulati*)	I. itch
10. सरदर्द (*sardard*)	J. vomit

Answers:

1. B	6. G
2. C	7. H
3. D	8. I
4. E	9. J
5. F	10. A

Health/सेहत

This staircase consists of a medicine related object on each step. Can you put the Hindi name of the object shown on each step?

Vegetables

सूई (sooee)............................ syringe
पट्टी(patti)............................ bandage
मरहम (maraham)................ ointment
बैसाखी (baisakhi)...................crutches
छड़ी(chadi)............................ cane
गोली (goli)............................ tablet

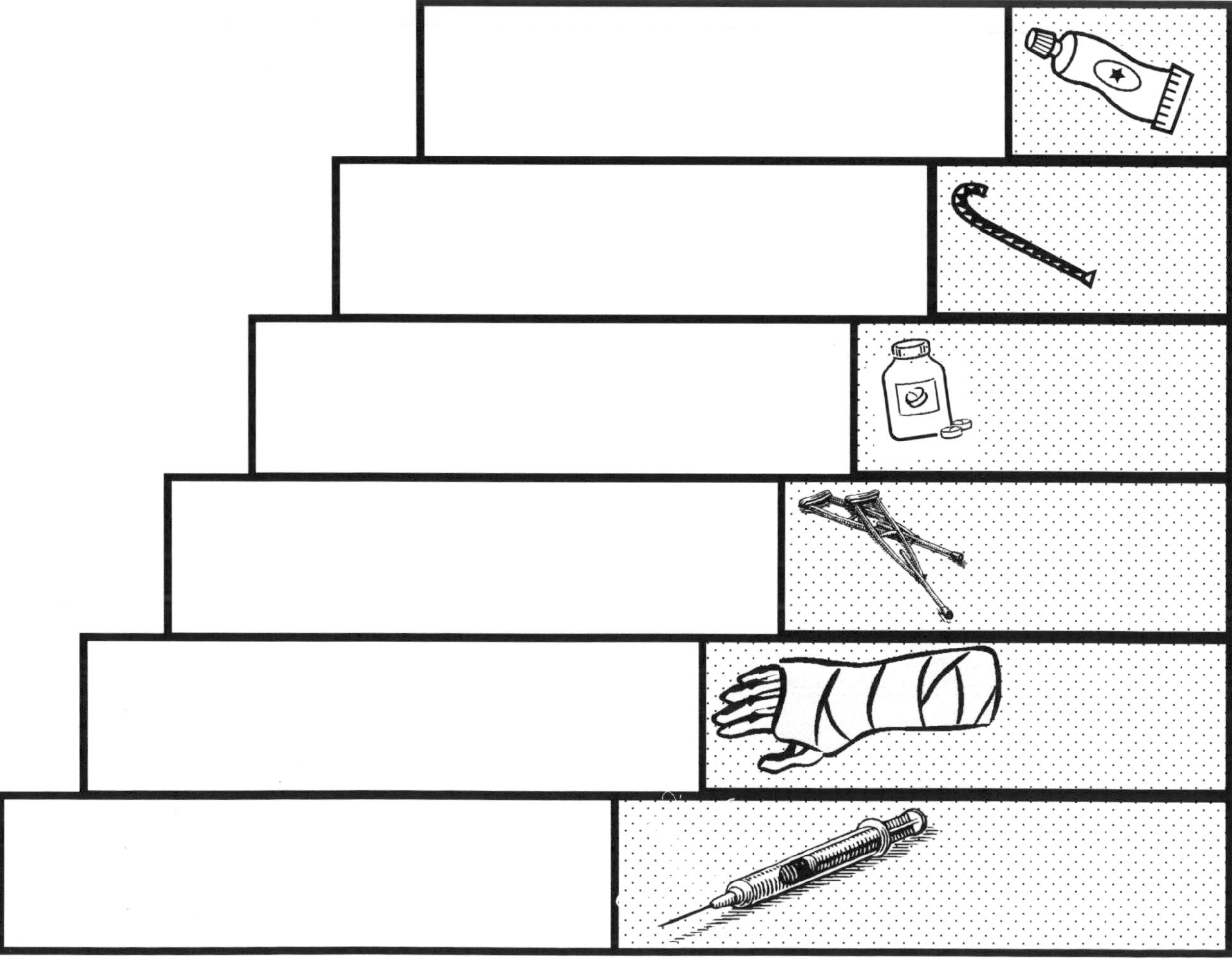

Health/सेहत

Match these words in Hindi with their English equivalent by drawing a line from the Hindi word to its corresponding English word.

Hindi	**English**
1. अस्पताल (*asptaal*)	A. pain
2. दवाखाना (*davakhana*)	B. hospital
3. डाक्टर (*doctor*)	C. massage
4. मालिश (*maalis*)	D. doctor
5. वैद्य(*vaidya*)	E. Traditional Muslim doctor
6. हकीम (*hakeem*)	F. Traditional Hindu doctor
7. दर्द (*dard*)	G. pharmacy
8. कब्ज (*kabj*)	H. accident
9. दुर्घटना (*durghatna*)	I. pimples
10. मुहांसे (*muhanse*)	J. constipation

Answers:

1. B	6.E
2. G	7. A
3. D	8. J
4. C	9. H
5. F	10. I

Arts/कला

On the lines in the inner wheel, write the numbers from the list below that gives the Hindi word matching with the English word on the outer wheel.

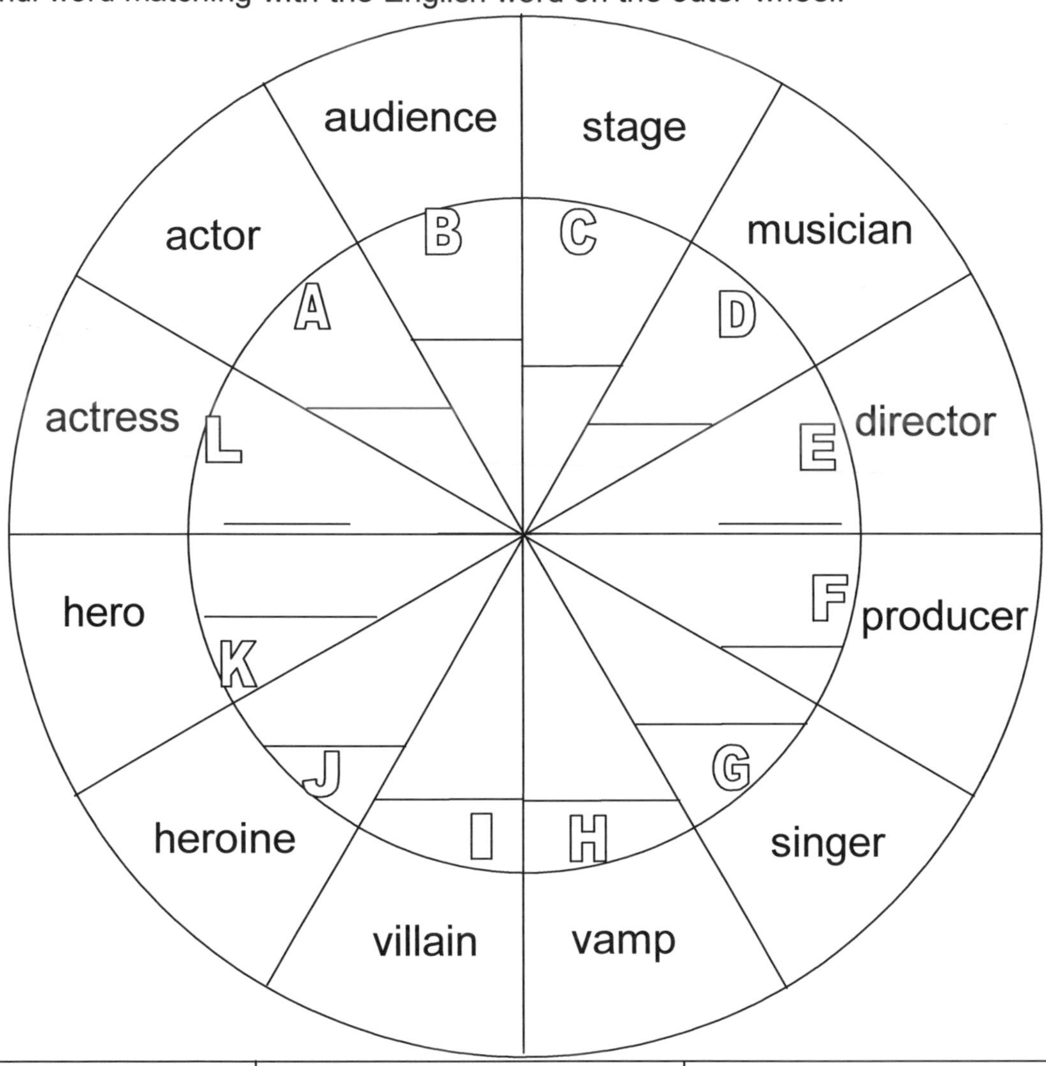

सूची (List)		
1. मंच (manch)	5. संगीतकार (sangeetkar)	9. नायिका (naaykia)
2. दर्शक (darshak)	6. निर्देशक (nirdeshak)	10. नायक (naayak)
3. अभिनेता (abhineta)	7. निर्माता (nirmata)	11.खलनायक (khalnayak)
4. अभिनेत्री (abhinetri)	8. गायक (gaayak)	12. खलनायिका (khalnayika)

Answers:

1. C	4. L	7. F	10. K
2. B	5. D	8. G	11. I
3. A	6. E	9. J	12. H

Arts/कला

Match these names for the different art related words with their pictures.

1. चित्र
(*chitra*)

2. चित्रकार
(*chitrakaar*)

3. तूलिका
(*tulikaa*)

4. रंग
(*rang*)

5. शिल्पी
(*shilipi*)

6. मूर्ति
(*murti*)

A. B.

C.

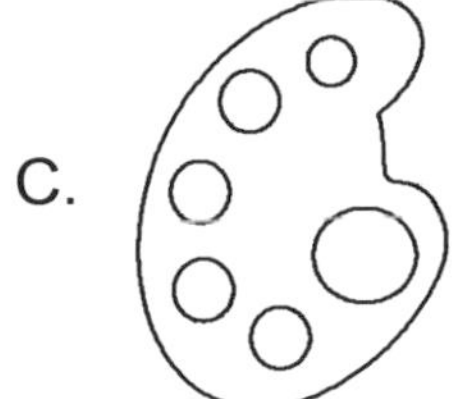

D.

E.

F.

Answers:
1. B (painting)
2. D (painter)
3. A (brush)
4. C (colors)
5. F (sculpture)
6. E (sculptor)

Emotions/भावना

Match these words in Hindi with their English equivalent by drawing a line from the Hindi word to its corresponding English word.

Hindi	English
1. खुश (*khush*)	A. sad
2. उदास (*udaas*)	B. tired
3. थका (*thakaa*)	C. happy
4. हारा (*haaraa*)	D. angry
5. गुस्सा(*gussa*)	E. defeated
6. रूवांसा (*rooaansa*)	F. naughty
7. चंचल (*chanchal*)	G. serious
8. गम्भीर (*gambhir*)	H. crying
9. रूठा (*roothaa*)	I. sleepy
10. उनीन्दा (*unindaa*)	J. upset

Answers:
1. C 2. A 3. B 4. E 5. D
6.H 7.F 8.G 9.J 10.I

Emotions/भावना

On the lines in the inner wheel, write the numbers from the list below that gives the name of the emotion written on the corresponding outer wheel.

सूची (List)		
1. पीड़ा (peeda)	5. प्यार (pyaar)	9. लज्जा (lajja)
2. आश्चर्य (aashcharya)	6. दया (daya)	10. उत्साह (utsaah)
3. चिंता (chinta)	7. संतोष (santosh)	11.भक्ती (bhakti)
4. डर (dar)	8. घृणा (ghrina)	12. गुस्सा (gussa)

Answers:
1. A
2. L
3. K
4. E
5. J
6. I
7. H
8. G
9. F
10. D
11. C
12. B

Festivals/त्यौहार

Match these names for the different art related words with their pictures.

1. होली
(*Holi*)

A. 

2. दिवाली
(*Diwali*)

B. 

3. राखी
(*Rakhee*)

C. 

4. ईद
(*Eid*)

D. 

5. जन्माष्टमी
(*Janmashtami*)

E. 

6. क्रिसमस
(*Christmas*)

F. 

Answers:
1. B (Holi)
2. A (Diwali)
3. D (Rakhee)
4. C (Eid)
5. F (Krishna's Birthday)
6. E (Christmas)

Actions/क्रिया

This staircase consists of an action shown on each step. Can you put the Hindi name of the activity shown on each step?

Actions

सोना (sona)............................ sleep
रोना (rona)............................. cry
खेलना (khelana)................ play
दौड़ना (dodhana)................... run
चलना (chalana)..................... walk
मुस्कराना (muskaraana)........ smile

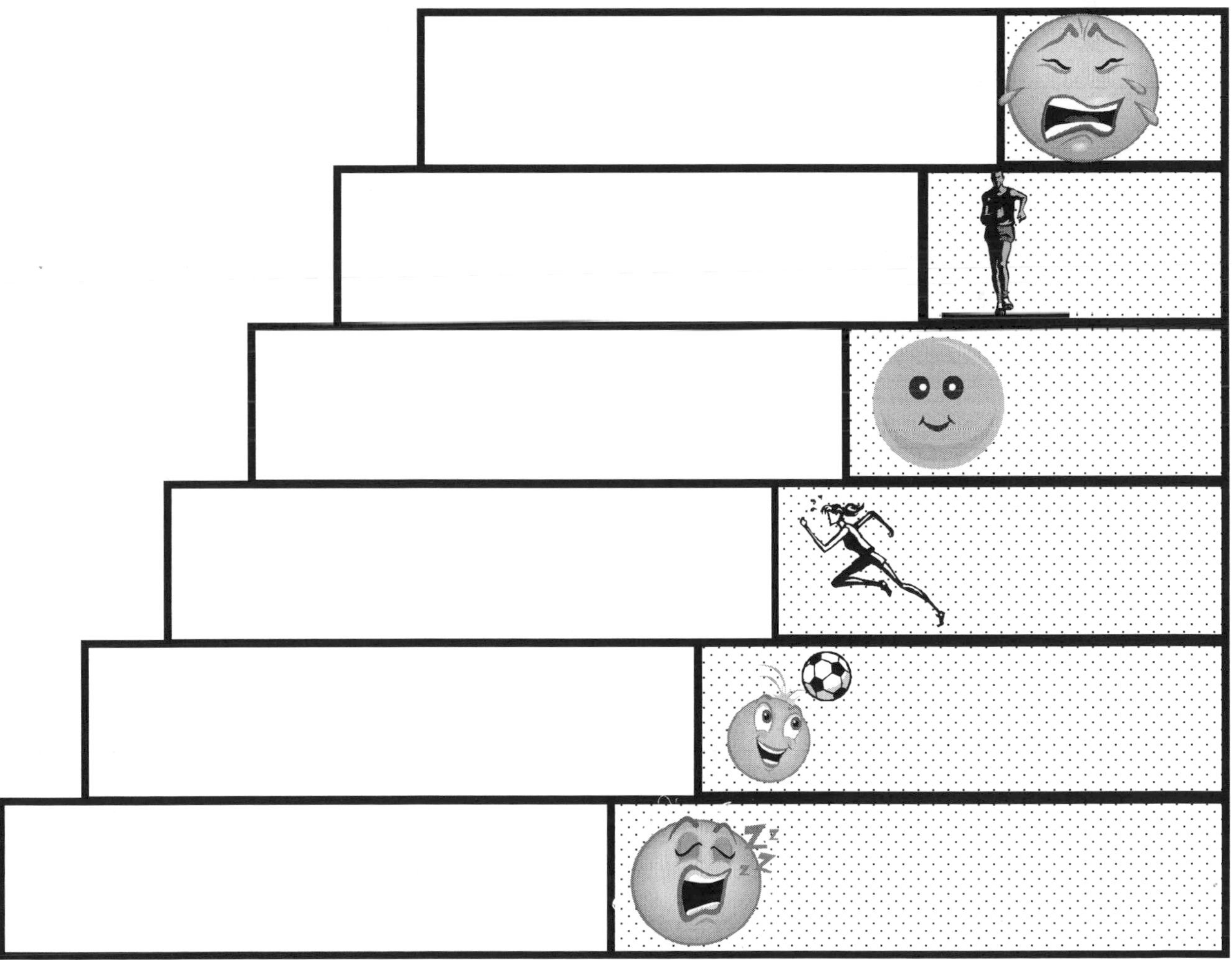

Actions/क्रिया

The action verbs below are hiding in this square. Find them. Circle them like the first word. Each word goes either top to bottom or left to right.

शब्द /Words

बोलना(bolanaa)	to speak	मिलना(milanaa)	to meet
खाना(khanaa)	to eat	टूटना(tootanaa)	to break
पीना(peenaa)	to drink	हंसना(hansanaa)	to laug
नहाना(nahaanaa)	to bathe	टहलना(tahalanaa)	to stroll
जागना(jaaganaa)	to wake	पहनना(pahananaa)	to wear
सुनना(sunanaa)	to hear	समझना(samajhanaa)	to understand
थकना(thakanaa)	to get tired	चहकना(chahakanaa)	to chirp
रुकना(rukanaa)	to stop	नाचना(nachanaa)	to dance
देखना(dekhanaa)	to see	डरना(daranaa)	to be scared
बताना(bataanaa)	to tell	पहचानना(pahachaananaa)	to recognize

पी	स	ना	का	रो	बो	क	च	स	च
ना	र	खा	ना	च	ल	ना	च	ता	को
व	लू	सो	न	हा	ना	मि	ल	ना	वा
जा	ग	ना	दे	क	र	सु	ट	च	प
र	रु	रो	ख	प	ह	न	ना	ना	ह
थ	क	ना	ना	मि	ल	ना	क	क	चा
चा	ना	ब	ता	ना	टू	र	स	ना	न
ट	ह	ल	ना	ह	ट	स	म	ड	ना
ना	प	ह	न	ना	ना	ना	झ	र	क
ठ	ह	र	ना	सौ	हं	स	ना	ना	ल

Metals/धातु

Match these metals written in Hindi with their English names by drawing a line between them.

Hindi	English
1. सोना (*sonaa*)	A. steel
2. चांदी (*chaandi*)	B. bronze
3. लोहा (*lohaa*)	C. gold
4. इसपात (*ispaat*)	D. iron
5. पीतल (*peetal*)	E. silver
6. ताम्बा (*taamba*)	F. brass
7. कांसा (*kaansaa*)	G. copper

Answers:
1. C
2. E
3. D
4. A
5. F
6. G
7. B

Metals/धातु

The rabbit needs to reach the carrot, but is only allowed to step on stones that are marked with iron or steel. Can you find a path for the rabbit to reach the carrot.

Answer: You can find a path using stones marked with the words लोहा (iron) or इसपात or फौलाद (both meaning steel).

Adjective/विशेषण

Match these words in Hindi with their English equivalent by drawing a line from the Hindi word to its corresponding English word.

Hindi	English
1. तेज (*tej*)	A. intelligent
2. सुस्त (*sust*)	B. foolish
3. बुद्धिमान (*buddhiman*)	C. fast
4. मूर्ख (*murkh*)	D. slow
5. अमीर (*ameer*)	E. poor
6. गरीब (*gareeb*)	F. rich
7. साफ (*saaf*)	G. light
8. गंदा (*ganda*)	H. heavy
9. हल्का (*halkaa*)	I. dirty
10. भारी (*bhaari*)	J. clean

Answers:

1.	C	6.	E
2.	D	7.	J
3.	A	8.	I
4.	B	9.	G
5.	F	10.	H

Adjective/विशेषण

This staircase consists of an adjective shown on each step. Can you put the Hindi name of the activity shown on each step?

Actions

बड़ा (bada)............................ big
छोटा (chhota)........................ small
मोटा (mota)........................ fat
पतला (patalaa).................. thin
लम्बा (lambaa)..................... tall
नाटा (naata)........................ short

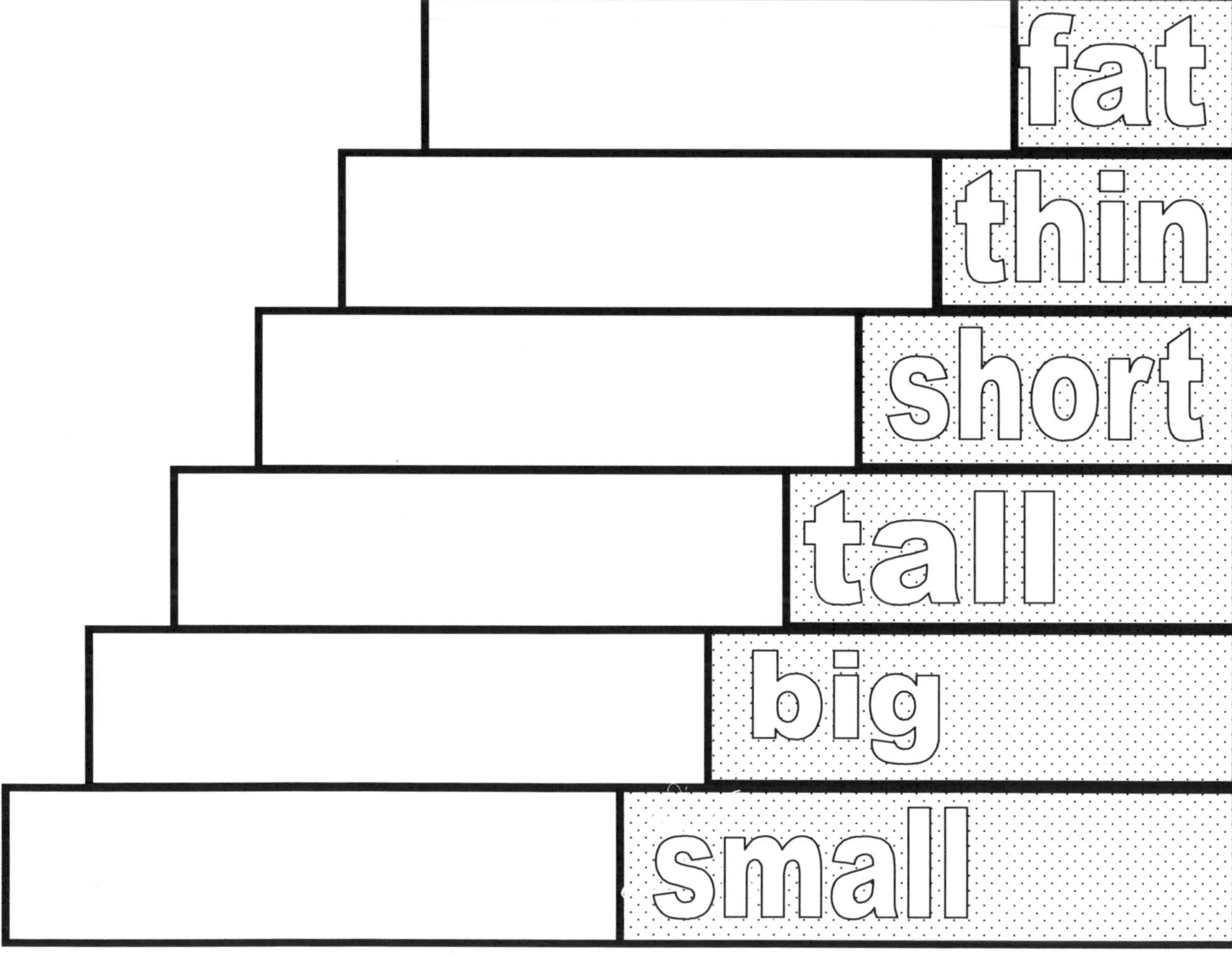

Adjective/विशेषण

Match these words in Hindi with their English equivalent by drawing a line from the Hindi word to its corresponding English word.

Hindi	English
1. सूखा (*sookha*)	A. high
2. गीला (*geelaa*)	B. dry
3. नीचा (*neecha*)	C. low
4. ऊँचा (*ooncha*)	D. wet
5. सच्चा (*saccha*)	E. liar
6. झूठा (*jhootha*)	F. old
7. पुराना (*puraanaa*)	G. truthful
8. नया (*nayaa*)	H. expensive
9. महंगा (*mahangaa*)	I. cheap
10. सस्ता (*sasta*)	J. new

Answers:

1. B	6. E
2. D	7. F
3. C	8. J
4. A	9. H
5. G	10. I

Imagination/कल्पना

Match these names for the different art related words with their pictures.

1. राजा (*Raaja*) — A.

2. रानी (*Raani*) — B.

3. भूत (*Bhoot*) — C.

4. जादूगर (*Jaadoogar*) — D.

5. परी (*paree*) — E.

6. राक्षस (*rakshasa*) — F.

Answers:
1. C (King)
2. A (Queen)
3. B (ghost)
4. F (Wizard)
5. D (fairy)
6. E (monster)

Imagination/कल्पना

Match these words in Hindi with their English equivalent by drawing a line from the Hindi word to its corresponding English word.

Hindi	English
1. जलपरी (*jalapari*)	A. palace
2. महल (*mahal*)	B. witch
3. चुड़ैल (*chudail*)	C. mermaid
4. दानव (*daanav*)	D. goblin
5. पिशाच (pisach)	E. giant
6. राजकुमार (*raajkumaar*)	F. angel
7. राजकुमारी (*raajkumaari*)	G. prince
8. फरिश्ता (*farishta*)	H. princess

Answers:
1. C
2. A
3. B
4. E
5. D
6. G
7. H
8. F

Direction/दिशा

On the lines in the inner wheel, write the numbers from the list below that gives the word written on the corresponding outer wheel.

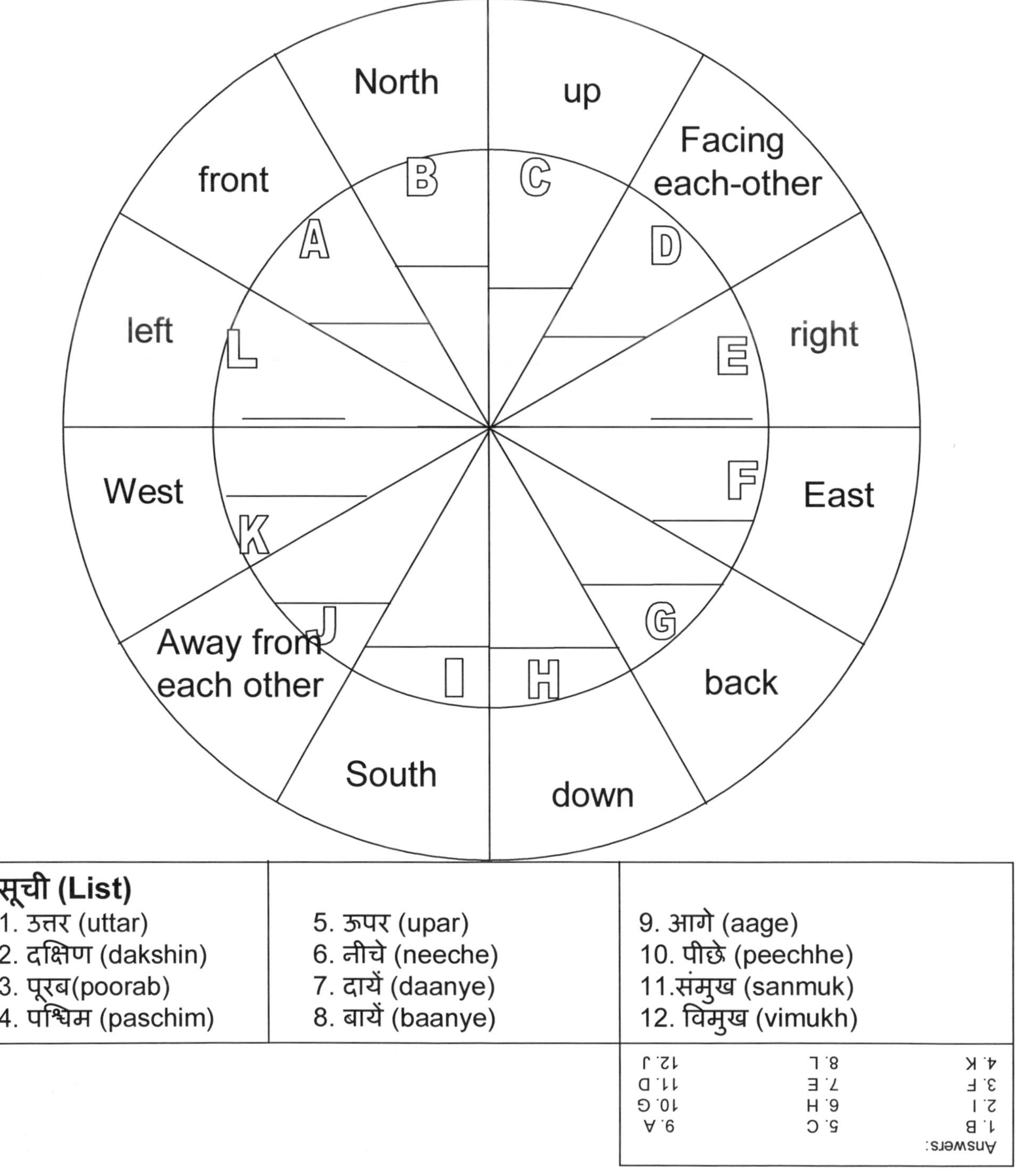

सूची (List)		
1. उत्तर (uttar)	5. ऊपर (upar)	9. आगे (aage)
2. दक्षिण (dakshin)	6. नीचे (neeche)	10. पीछे (peechhe)
3. पूरब(poorab)	7. दायें (daanye)	11.संमुख (sanmuk)
4. पश्चिम (paschim)	8. बायें (baanye)	12. विमुख (vimukh)

Answers:

1. B	5. C	9. A
2. I	6. H	10. G
3. F	7. E	11. D
4. K	8. L	12. J

War/लड़ाई

Match these words for different types of jobs with their pictures.

1.बंदूक (*bandook*)	A. 
2. तोप (*top*)	B.
3. तलवार (*talavaar*)	C. 
4. तीर (*teer*)	D. 
5. धनुष (*dhanush*)	E. 
6. भाला (*bhaalaa*)	F.

Answers:

1.	B (gun)	4.F(arrow)	
2.	A (canon)	5. C (bow)	
3.	D (sword)	6. E (spear)	

War/लड़ाई

Match these words in Hindi with their English equivalent by drawing a line from the Hindi word to its corresponding English word.

Hindi	English
1. सेना (*sena*)	A. soldier
2. नौसेना (*nausena*)	B. army
3. वायुसेना (*vayusena*)	C. navy
4. सैनिक (*sainik*)	D. air-force
5. सेनापति (*senapati*)	E. platoon
6. पलटन (*palatan*)	F. captain
7. कप्तान (*kaptaan*)	G. Commanding General
8. बम (*bum*)	H. submarine
9. पनडुब्बी(*panadubbi*)	I. spy
10. जासूस(*jasoos*)	J. bomb

Answers:

1.	B	6.	E
2.	C	7.	F
3.	D	8.	J
4.	A	9.	H
5.	G	10.	I

Sports/खेल

The sports words below are hiding in this square. Find them. Circle them like the first word. Each word goes either top to bottom or left to right.

शब्द /Words

गेंद (gaind)	ball	हार (haar)	defeat
बल्ला (balla)	bat	विजेता (vijeta)	winner
मैदान (maidan)	field	टीम (team)	team
दौड़ (daud)	race	कप्तान (kaptan)	captain
आँखमिचौली (aankh-michauli)	hide&seek	अखाड़ा (akhada)	arena
कबड्डी(kabaddi)	kabaddi	कुश्ती (kushti)	wrestling
खेल (khel)	play	तैराकी (tairaki)	swimming
खिलाड़ी (khiladi)	player	चुनौती (chunauti)	challenge
अनाड़ी (anadi)	novice player	तीरंदाजी(hans)	archery
जीत (jeet)	victory	नतीजा (nateeja)	result

जी	रा	हा	पि	गें	द	न	स	क	चु
त	ट	र	क	ह	र	द	म	स	नौ
ट	ब	ल्ला	गी	जी	ला	ड़ी	तू	क	ती
ल	न	बी	न	मै	दा	न	ती	जा	च
क	ब	ड्	डी	का	कि	स्सा	कि	खे	ल
ती	र	ध	नु	अ	खा	ड़ा	स	क	ल
तै	रा	की	म	ना	ग	ल	कु	श्ती	दा
य	क	खि	ला	ड़ी	र	घु	ना	य	क
गु	न	ती	रं	दा	जी	गा	न	सा	प्ता
वि	जे	ता	द	टी	म	र	सु	न	न

Sports/खेल

Match these words for different types of jobs with their pictures.

1. गोली
(*goli*)

A. 

2. ताश
(*taash*)

B. 

3. पांसा
(*paansa*)

C. 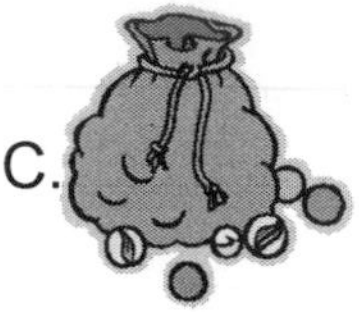

4. शतरंज
(*shataranj*)

D. 

5. मोहरा
(*moharaa*)

E. 

6. गुड़िया
(*gudiya*)

F. 

Answers:
1. C (marbles) 4. E (chess)
2. A (cards) 5. F (chess-piece)
3. B (dice) 6. D (doll)

Conjugations

The next few pages of this book demonstrate the conjugations of different letters in the Hindi alphabet. The first two pages list the table that show how the matras are applied to different letters. This is followed by a summary of the rules of combining consonants together. The following pages show how different consonants can be combined together.

Conjugations

The table below shows the consonants from क - न conjugated with the 13 vowels.

	अ	आ	इ	ई	उ	ऊ	ऋ	ए	ऐ	ओ	औ	अं	अः
क	क	का	कि	की	कु	कू	कृ	के	कै	को	कौ	कं	कः
ख	ख	खा	खि	खी	खु	खू	खृ	खे	खै	खो	खौ	खं	खः
ग	ग	गा	गि	गी	गु	गू	गृ	गे	गै	गो	गौ	गं	गः
घ	घ	घा	घि	घी	घु	घू	घृ	घे	घै	घो	घौ	घं	घः
ङ	ङ	ङा	ङि	ङी	ङु	ङू	ङृ	ङे	ङै	ङो	ङौ	ङं	ङः
च	च	चा	चि	ची	चु	चू	चृ	चे	चै	चो	चौ	चं	चः
छ	छ	छा	छि	छी	छु	छू	छृ	छे	छै	छो	छौ	छं	छः
ज	ज	जा	जि	जी	जु	जू	जृ	जे	जै	जो	जौ	जं	जः
झ	झ	झा	झि	झी	झु	झू	झृ	झे	झै	झो	झौ	झं	झः
ञ	ञ	ञा	ञि	ञी	ञु	ञू	ञृ	ञे	ञै	ञो	ञौ	ञं	ञः
ट	ट	टा	टि	टी	टु	टू	टृ	टे	टै	टो	टौ	टं	टः
ठ	ठ	ठा	ठि	ठी	ठु	ठू	ठृ	ठे	ठै	ठो	ठौ	ठं	ठः
ड	ड	डा	डि	डी	डु	डू	डृ	डे	डै	डो	डौ	डं	डः
ढ	ढ	ढा	ढि	ढी	ढु	ढू	ढृ	ढे	ढै	ढो	ढौ	ढं	ढः
ण	ण	णा	णि	णी	णु	णू	णृ	णे	णै	णो	णौ	णं	णः
त	त	ता	ति	ती	तु	तू	तृ	ते	तै	तो	तौ	तं	तः
थ	थ	था	थि	थी	थु	थू	थृ	थे	थै	थो	थौ	थं	थः
द	द	दा	दि	दी	दु	दू	दृ	दे	दै	दो	दौ	दं	दः
ध	ध	धा	धि	धी	धु	धू	धृ	धे	धै	धो	धौ	धं	धः
न	न	ना	नि	नी	नु	नू	नृ	ने	नै	नो	नौ	नं	नः

Conjugations

The table below shows the shapes consonants प- ह and some special combined consonants conjugated with the 13 vowels.

	अ	आ	इ	ई	उ	ऊ	ऋ	ए	ऐ	ओ	औ	अं	अः
प	प	पा	पि	पी	पु	पू	पृ	पे	पै	पो	पौ	पं	पः
फ	फ	फा	फि	फी	फु	फू	फृ	फे	फै	फो	फौ	फं	फः
ब	ब	बा	बि	बी	बु	बू	बृ	बे	बै	बो	बौ	ब	बः
भ	भ	भा	भि	भी	भु	भू	भृ	भे	भै	भो	भौ	भं	भः
म	म	मा	मि	मी	मु	मू	मृ	मे	मै	मो	मौ	मं	मः
य	य	या	यि	यी	यु	यू	यृ	ये	यै	यो	यौ	यं	यः
र	र	रा	रि	री	रु	रू	रृ	रे	रै	रो	रौ	रं	रः
ल	ल	ला	लि	ली	लु	लू	लृ	ले	लै	लो	लौ	लं	लः
व	व	वा	वि	वी	वु	वू	वृ	वे	वै	वो	वौ	वं	वः
श	श	शा	शि	शी	शु	शू	शृ	शे	शै	शो	शौ	शं	शः
ष	ष	षा	षि	षी	षु	षू	षृ	षे	षै	षो	षौ	षं	षः
स	स	सा	सि	सी	सु	सू	सृ	से	सै	सो	सौ	सं	सः
ह	ह	हा	हि	ही	हु	हू	हृ	हे	है	हो	हौ	हं	हः
क्ष	क्ष	क्षा	क्षि	क्षी	क्षु	क्षू	क्षृ	क्षे	क्षै	क्षो	क्षौ	क्षं	क्षः
त्र	त्र	त्रा	त्रि	त्री	त्रु	त्रू	त्रृ	त्रे	त्रै	त्रो	त्रौ	त्रं	त्र
ज्ञ	ज्ञ	ज्ञा	ज्ञि	ज्ञी	ज्ञु	ज्ञू	ज्ञृ	ज्ञे	ज्ञै	ज्ञो	ज्ञौ	ज्ञं	ज्ञः
श्र	श्र	श्रा	श्रि	श्री	श्रु	श्रू	श्रृ	श्रे	श्रै	श्रो	श्रौ	श्रं	श्रः

Conjugations
Constant Combination Rules

Consonants can be combined with each other. Usually half a constant is shown by the oblique line below it, e.g. क् mean one half of the क sound. The half consonant is combined with the following consonant and the combined consonant has a new form. The following are the rules used to determine how to make the combined consonants from two consonants. The combined consonant can take matras like the regular consonants.

Any consonant with a vertical line at end loses that line if you only want half of it.

क् + य = क्य	न् + य = न्य	ग् + त = ग्त
ज् + व = ज्व	ब् + स = ब्स	च् + य = च्य

When you add half of र to another letter, it shows up as a mark on top of that letter.

र् + य = र्य	र् + क = र्क	र् + ज = र्ज
र् + व = र्व	र् + स = र्स	र् + ह = र्ह

When you add half a letter with a vertical line to र , it shows as an oblique mark on the letter.

य् + र = य्र	व् + र = व्र	क् + र = क्र
प् + र = प्र	स् + र = स्र	ग् + र = ग्र

When you add half of other letters to र , it shows as two marks under that letter.

ट्+ र = ट्र	ठ् + र = ठ्र	ढ् + र = ढ्र

The complete table for creating combined consonants is shown in the next four pages.

Conjugations

The table below shows the combination of the consonants from क- न with themselves. Each entry shows the new combined consonant when half of the consonant in the first column is combined with the consonant in the top row. For example, क् +त = क्त.

	क	ख	ग	घ	ङ	च	छ	ज	झ	ञ	ट	ठ	ड	ढ	ण	त	थ	द	ध	न
क	क्क	क्ख	क्ग	क्घ	क्ङ	क्च	क्छ	क्ज	क्झ	क्ञ	क्ट	क्ठ	क्ड	क्ढ	क्ण	क्त	क्थ	क्द	क्ध	क्न
ख	ख्क	ख्ख	ख्ग	ख्घ	ख्ङ	ख्च	ख्छ	ख्ज	ख्झ	ख्ञ	ख्ट	ख्ठ	ख्ड	ख्ढ	ख्ण	ख्त	ख्थ	ख्द	ख्ध	ख्न
ग	ग्क	ग्ख	ग्ग	ग्घ	ग्ङ	ग्च	ग्छ	ग्ज	ग्झ	ग्ञ	ग्ट	ग्ठ	ग्ड	ग्ढ	ग्ण	ग्त	ग्थ	ग्द	ग्ध	ग्न
घ	घ्क	घ्ख	घ्ग	घ्घ	घ्ङ	घ्च	घ्छ	घ्ज	घ्झ	घ्ञ	घ्ट	घ्ठ	घ्ड	घ्ढ	घ्ण	घ्त	घ्थ	घ्द	घ्ध	घ्न
ङ	ङ्क	ङ्ख	ङ्ग	ङ्घ	ङ्ङ	ङ्च	ङ्छ	ङ्ज	ङ्झ	ङ्ञ	ङ्ट	ङ्ठ	ङ्ड	ङ्ढ	ङ्ण	ङ्त	ङ्थ	ङ्द	ङ्ध	ङ्न
च	च्क	च्ख	च्ग	च्घ	च्ङ	च्च	च्छ	च्ज	च्झ	च्ञ	च्ट	च्ठ	च्ड	च्ढ	च्ण	च्त	च्थ	च्द	च्ध	च्न
छ	छ्क	छ्ख	छ्ग	छ्घ	छ्ङ	छ्च	छ्छ	छ्ज	छ्झ	छ्ञ	छ्ट	छ्ठ	छ्ड	छ्ढ	छ्ण	छ्त	छ्थ	छ्द	छ्ध	छ्न
ज	ज्क	ज्ख	ज्ग	ज्घ	ज्ङ	ज्च	ज्छ	ज्ज	ज्झ	ज्ञ	ज्ट	ज्ठ	ज्ड	ज्ढ	ज्ण	ज्त	ज्थ	ज्द	ज्ध	ज्न
झ	झ्क	झ्ख	झ्ग	झ्घ	झ्ङ	झ्च	झ्छ	झ्ज	झ्झ	झ्ञ	झ्ट	झ्ठ	झ्ड	झ्ढ	झ्ण	झ्त	झ्थ	झ्द	झ्ध	झ्न
ञ	ञ्क	ञ्ख	ञ्ग	ञ्घ	ञ्ङ	ञ्च	ञ्छ	ञ्ज	ञ्झ	ञ्ञ	ञ्ट	ञ्ठ	ञ्ड	ञ्ढ	ञ्ण	ञ्त	ञ्थ	ञ्द	ञ्ध	ञ्न
ट	ट्क	ट्ख	ट्ग	ट्घ	ट्ङ	ट्च	ट्छ	ट्ज	ट्झ	ट्ञ	ट्ट	ट्ठ	ट्ड	ट्ढ	ट्ण	ट्त	ट्थ	ट्द	ट्ध	ट्न
ठ	ठ्क	ठ्ख	ठ्ग	ठ्घ	ठ्ङ	ठ्च	ठ्छ	ठ्ज	ठ्झ	ठ्ञ	ठ्ट	ठ्ठ	ठ्ड	ठ्ढ	ठ्ण	ठ्त	ठ्थ	ठ्द	ठ्ध	ठ्न
ड	ड्क	ड्ख	ड्ग	ड्घ	ड्ङ	ड्च	ड्छ	ड्ज	ड्झ	ड्ञ	ड्ट	ड्ठ	ड्ड	ड्ढ	ड्ण	ड्त	ड्थ	ड्द	ड्ध	ड्न
ढ	ढ्क	ढ्ख	ढ्ग	ढ्घ	ढ्ङ	ढ्च	ढ्छ	ढ्ज	ढ्झ	ढ्ञ	ढ्ट	ढ्ठ	ढ्ड	ढ्ढ	ढ्ण	ढ्त	ढ्थ	ढ्द	ढ्ध	ढ्न
ण	ण्क	ण्ख	ण्ग	ण्घ	ण्ङ	ण्च	ण्छ	ण्ज	ण्झ	ण्ञ	ण्ट	ण्ठ	ण्ड	ण्ढ	ण्ण	ण्त	ण्थ	ण्द	ण्ध	ण्न
त	त्क	त्ख	त्ग	त्घ	त्ङ	त्च	त्छ	त्ज	त्झ	त्ञ	त्ट	त्ठ	त्ड	त्ढ	त्ण	त्त	त्थ	त्द	त्ध	त्न
थ	थ्क	थ्ख	थ्ग	थ्घ	थ्ङ	थ्च	थ्छ	थ्ज	थ्झ	थ्ञ	थ्ट	थ्ठ	थ्ड	थ्ढ	थ्ण	थ्त	थ्थ	थ्द	थ्ध	थ्न
द	द्क	द्ख	द्ग	द्घ	द्ङ	द्च	द्छ	द्ज	द्झ	द्ञ	द्ट	द्ठ	द्ड	द्ढ	द्ण	द्त	द्थ	द्द	द्ध	द्न
ध	ध्क	ध्ख	ध्ग	ध्ग	ध्ङ	ध्च	ध्छ	ध्ज	ध्झ	ध्ञ	ध्ट	ध्ठ	ध्ड	ध्ढ	ध्ण	ध्त	ध्थ	ध्द	ध्ध	ध्न
न	न्क	न्ख	न्ग	न्घ	न्ङ	न्च	न्छ	न्ज	न्झ	न्ञ	न्ट	न्ठ	न्ड	न्ढ	न्ण	न्त	न्थ	न्द	न्ध	न्न

Conjugations

The table below shows the combination of the consonants from क- न with प- ह. Each entry shows the new combined consonant when half of the consonant in the first column is combined with the consonant in the top row. For example, क् + र = क्र.

	प	फ	ब	भ	म	य	र	ल	व	श	ष	स	ह
क	क्प	क्फ	क्ब	क्भ	क्म	क्य	क्र	क्ल	क्व	क्श	क्ष	क्स	क्ह
ख	ख्प	ख्फ	ख्ब	ख्भ	ख्म	ख्य	ख्र	ख्ल	ख्व	ख्श	ख्ष	ख्स	ख्ह
ग	ग्प	ग्फ	ग्ब	ग्भ	ग्म	ग्य	ग्र	ग्ल	ग्व	ग्श	ग्ष	ग्स	ग्ह
घ	घ्प	घ्फ	घ्ब	घ्भ	घ्म	घ्य	घ्र	घ्ल	घ्व	घ्श	घ्ष	घ्स	घ्ह
ङ	ङ्प	ङ्फ	ङ्ब	ङ्भ	ङ्म	ङ्य	ङ्र	ङ्ल	ङ्व	ङ्श	ङ्ष	ङ्स	ङ्ह
च	च्प	च्फ	च्ब	च्भ	च्म	च्य	च्र	च्ल	च्व	च्श	च्ष	च्स	च्ह
छ	छ्प	छ्फ	छ्ब	छ्भ	छ्म	छ्य	छ्र	छ्ल	छ्व	छ्श	छ्	छ्स	छ्ह
ज	ज्प	ज्फ	ज्ब	ज्भ	ज्म	ज्य	ज्र	ज्ल	ज्व	ज्श	ज्ष	ज्स	ज्ह
झ	झ्प	झ्फ	झ्ब	झ्भ	झ्म	झ्य	झ्र	झ्ल	झ्व	झ्श	झ्ष	झ्स	झ्ह
ञ	ञ्प	ञ्फ	ञ्ब	ञ्भ	ञ्म	ञ्य	ञ्र	ञ्ल	ञ्व	ञ्श	ञ्ष	ञ्स	ञ्ह
ट	ट्प	ट्फ	ट्ब	ट्भ	ट्म	ट्य	ट्र	ट्ल	ट्व	ट्श	ट्ष	ट्स	ट्ह
ठ	ठ्प	ठ्फ	ठ्ब	ठ्भ	ठ्म	ठ्य	ठ्र	ठ्ल	ठ्व	ठ्श	ठ्ष	ठ्स	ठ्ह
ड	ड्प	ड्फ	ड्ब	ड्भ	ड्म	ड्य	ड्र	ड्ल	ड्व	ड्श	ड्ष	ड्स	ड्ह
ढ	ढ्प	ढ्फ	ढ्ब	ढ्भ	ढ्म	ढ्य	ढ्र	ढ्ल	ढ्व	ढ्श	ढ्ष	ढ्स	ढ्ह
ण	ण्प	ण्फ	ण्ब	ण्भ	ण्म	ण्य	ण्र	ण्ल	ण्व	ण्श	ण्ष	ण्स	ण्ह
त	त्प	त्फ	त्ब	त्भ	त्म	त्य	त्र	त्ल	त्व	त्श	त्ष	त्स	त्ह
थ	थ्प	थ्फ	थ्ब	थ्भ	थ्म	थ्य	थ्र	थ्ल	थ्व	थ्श	थ्ष	थ्स	थ्ह
द	द्प	द्फ	द्ब	द्भ	द्म	द्य	द्र	द्ल	द्व	द्श	द्ष	द्स	द्ह
ध	ध्प	ध्फ	ध्ब	ध्भ	ध्म	ध्य	ध्र	ध्ल	ध्व	ध्श	ध्ष	ध्स	ध्ह
न	न्प	न्फ	न्ब	न्भ	न्म	न्य	न्र	न्ल	न्व	न्श	न्ष	न्स	न्ह

Conjugations

The table below shows the combination of the consonants from प- ह with क- न. Each entry shows the new combined consonant when half of the consonant in the first column is combined with the consonant in the top row. For example, र् + क = र्क.

	क	ख	ग	घ	ङ	च	छ	ज	झ	ञ	ट	ठ	ड	ढ	ण	त	थ	द	ध	न
प	प्क	प्ख	प्ग	प्घ	प्ङ	प्च	प्छ	प्ज	प्झ	प्ञ	प्ट	प्ठ	प्ड	प्ढ	प्ण	प्त	प्थ	प्द	प्ध	प्न
फ	फ्क	फ्ख	फ्ग	फ्घ	फ्ङ	फ्च	फ्छ	फ्ज	फ्झ	फ्ञ	फ्ट	फ्ठ	फ्ड	फ्ढ	फ्ण	फ्त	फ्थ	फ्द	फ्ध	फ्न
ब	ब्क	ब्ख	ब्ग	ब्घ	ब्ङ	ब्च	ब्छ	ब्ज	ब्झ	ब्ञ	ब्ट	ब्ठ	ब्ड	ब्ढ	ब्ण	ब्त	ब्थ	ब्द	ब्ध	ब्न
भ	भ्क	भ्ख	भ्ग	भ्घ	भ्ङ	भ्च	भ्छ	भ्ज	भ्झ	भ्ञ	भ्ट	भ्ठ	भ्ड	भ्ढ	भ्ण	भ्त	भ्थ	भ्द	भ्ध	भ्न
म	म्क	म्ख	म्ग	म्घ	म्ङ	म्च	म्छ	म्ज	म्झ	म्ञ	म्ट	म्ठ	म्ड	म्ढ	म्ण	म्त	म्थ	म्द	म्ध	म्न
य	य्क	य्ख	य्ग	य्घ	य्ङ	य्च	य्छ	य्ज	य्झ	य्ञ	य्ट	य्ठ	य्ड	य्ढ	य्ण	य्त	य्थ	य्द	य्ध	य्न
र	र्क	र्ख	र्ग	र्घ	र्ङ	र्च	र्छ	र्ज	र्झ	र्ञ	र्ट	र्ठ	र्ड	र्ढ	र्ण	र्त	र्थ	र्द	र्ध	र्न
ल	ल्क	ल्ख	ल्ग	ल्घ	ल्ङ	ल्च	ल्छ	ल्ज	ल्झ	ल्ञ	ल्ट	ल्ठ	ल्ड	ल्ढ	ल्ण	ल्त	ल्थ	ल्द	ल्ध	ल्न
व	व्क	व्ख	व्ग	व्घ	व्ङ	व्च	व्छ	व्ज	व्झ	व्ञ	व्ट	व्ठ	व्ड	व्ढ	व्ण	व्त	व्थ	व्द	व्ध	व्न
श	श्क	श्ख	श्ग	श्घ	श्ङ	श्च	श्छ	श्ज	श्झ	श्ञ	श्ट	श्ठ	श्ड	श्ढ	श्ण	श्त	श्थ	श्द	श्झ	श्न
ष	ष्क	ष्ख	ष्ग	ष्घ	ष्ङ	ष्च	ष्छ	ष्ज	ष्झ	ष्ञ	ष्ट	ष्ठ	ष्ड	ष्ढ	ष्ण	ष्त	ष्थ	ष्द	ष्ध	ष्न
स	स्क	स्ख	स्ग	स्घ	स्ङ	स्च	स्छ	स्ज	स्झ	स्ञ	स्ट	स्ठ	स्ड	स्ढ	स्ण	स्त	स्थ	स्द	स्ध	स्न
ह	ह्क	ह्ख	ह्ग	ह्घ	ह्ङ	ह्च	ह्छ	ह्ज	ह्झ	ह्ञ	ह्ट	ह्ठ	ह्ड	ह्ढ	ह्ण	ह्त	ह्थ	ह्द	ह्ध	ह्न

Conjugations

The table below shows the combination of the consonants from प- ह with क- न. Each entry shows the new combined consonant when half of the consonant in the first column is combined with the consonant in the top row. For example, र् + प = र्प.

	प	फ	ब	भ	म	य	र	ल	व	श	ष	स	ह
प	प्प	प्फ	प्ब	प्भ	प्म	प्य	प्र	प्ल	प्व	प्श	प्ष	प्स	प्ह
फ	फ्प	फ्फ	फ्ब	फ्भ	फ्म	फ्य	फ्र	फ्ल	फ्व	फ्श	फ्ष	फ्स	फ्ह
ब	ब्प	ब्फ	ब्ब	ब्भ	ब्म	ब्य	ब्र	ब्ल	ब्व	ब्श	ब्ष	ब्स	ब्ह
भ	भ्प	भ्फ	भ्ब	भ्भ	भ्म	भ्य	भ्र	भ्ल	भ्व	भ्श	भ्ष	भ्स	भ्ह
म	म्प	म्फ	म्ब	म्भ	म्म	म्य	म्र	म्ल	म्व	म्श	म्ष	म्स	म्ह
य	य्प	य्फ	य्ब	य्भ	य्म	य्य	य्र	य्ल	य्व	य्श	य्ष	य्स	य्ह
र	र्प	र्फ	र्ब	र्भ	र्म	र्य	र्र	र्ल	र्व	र्श	र्ष	र्स	र्ह
ल	ल्प	ल्फ	ल्ब	ल्भ	ल्म	ल्य	ल्र	ल्ल	ल्व	ल्श	ल्ष	ल्स	ल्ह
व	व्प	व्फ	व्ब	व्भ	व्म	व्य	व्र	व्ल	व्व	व्श	व्ष	व्स	व्ह
श	श्प	श्फ	श्ब	श्भ	श्म	श्य	श्र	श्ल	श्व	श्श	श्ष	श्स	श्ह
ष	ष्प	ष्फ	ष्ब	ष्भ	ष्म	ष्य	ष्र	ष्ल	ष्व	ष्श	ष्ष	ष्स	ष्ह
स	स्प	स्फ	स्ब	स्भ	स्म	स्य	स्र	स्ल	स्व	स्श	स्ष	स्स	स्ह
ह	ह्प	ह्फ	ह्ब	ह्भ	ह्म	ह्य	ह्र	ह्ल	ह्व	ह्श	ह्ष	ह्स	ह्ह

Publications of Chanda Books

Level 1 Hindi:

Aamoo the Aam
Aamoo the Aam – Part II
Aamoo the Aam – Part III
Hindi Children's Book Level 1 Easy Reader

Level 2 Hindi:

Tara Sitara
Tara ke Kisse
Hindi Children's Book Level 2 Easy Reader

Level 3 Hindi:

Sonu ke Kisse
Sonu ke Afsane
Sonu ke Tyohar
Hindi Children's Book Level 3 Easy Reader

Activity Books:

Learn Hindi Alphabet Activity Workbook
Learn Hindi Vocabulary Activity Workbook
Learn Hindi Grammar Activity Workbook
Hindi Activity Workbook
Hinduism for Children Activity Workbook
Learn Bengali Alphabet Activity Workbook
Learn Bengali Vocabulary Activity Workbook

Alphabet Books:

Bengali Alphabet Book
Gujarati Alphabet Book
Hindi Alphabet Book
Marathi Alphabet Book
Punjabi Alphabet Book

Others:

Bhajan Ganga
Indian Culture Stories: Sanskar
South Asian Immigration Stories

For an updated list, visit us at http://www.chandabooks.com